MW01055309

CAMPAIGN 282

LEYTE 1944

Return to the Philippines

CLAYTON K. S. CHUN

ILLUSTRATED BY GIUSEPPE RAVA
Series editor Marcus Cowper

First published in Great Britain in 2015 by Osprey Publishing,
PO Box 883, Oxford, OX1 9PL, UK
PO Box 3985, New York, NY 10185-3985, USA
E-mail: info@ospreypublishing.com

© 2015 Osprey Publishing Ltd
OSPREY PUBLISHING IS PART OF THE BLOOMSBURY PUBLISHING LTD.

All rights reserved. Apart from any fair dealing for the purpose of private
study, research, criticism or review, as permitted under the Copyright,
Designs and Patents Act, 1988, no part of this publication may be
reproduced, stored in a retrieval system, or transmitted in any form or by
any means, electronic, electrical, chemical, mechanical, optical,
photocopying, recording or otherwise, without the prior written permission
of the copyright owner. Enquiries should be addressed to the Publishers.

A CIP catalog record for this book is available from the British Library.

ISBN: 978 1 4728 0690 1
PDF e-book ISBN: 978 1 4728 0691 8
e-Pub ISBN: 978 1 4728 0692 5

Editorial by Ilios Publishing Ltd, Oxford, UK (www.iliospublishing.com)
Index by Mark Swift
Typeset in Myriad Pro and Sabon
Maps by Bounford.com
3D bird's-eye views by The Black Spot
Battlescene illustrations by Giuseppe Rava
Originated by PDQ Media, Bungay, UK
Printed in China through Worldprint Ltd.

15 16 17 18 19   10 9 8 7 6 5 4 3 2 1

ARTIST'S NOTE

Readers may care to note that the original paintings from which the color
plates in this book were prepared are available for private sale. The
Publishers retain all reproduction copyright whatsoever. The artist can be
contacted via the following website:
www.g-rava.it
The Publishers regret that they can enter into no correspondence upon this
matter.

THE WOODLAND TRUST

Osprey Publishing are supporting the Woodland Trust, the UK's leading
woodland conservation charity, by funding the dedication of trees.

LIST OF ACRONYMS AND ABBREVIATIONS

AA	anti-aircraft
ASC	Army Service Command
CCS	Combined Chiefs of Staff
CD	cavalry division (US)
CMH	Congressional Medal of Honor
CVE	escort carrier
FEAF	Far East Air Forces
GHQ	General Headquarters
ID	infantry division (US)
IGHQ	Imperial General Headquarters
IJA	Imperial Japanese Army
IJAAF	Imperial Japanese Army Air Forces
IJN	Imperial Japanese Navy
IJNAF	Imperial Japanese Navy Air Forces
IMB	independent mixed brigade (Japan)
JCS	Joint Chiefs of Staff
LCI	landing craft, infantry
LSM	landing ship, medium
LST	landing ship, tank
LVT	landing vehicle, tracked
POA	Pacific Ocean Area
RAAF	Royal Australian Air Force
RCT	Regimental Combat Team
SWPA	Southwest Pacific Area
TF	task force
TG	task group
USAAF	United States Army Air Forces
USAFFE	US Army Forces in the Far East
USMA	US Military Academy
USN	US Navy

ACKNOWLEDGEMENTS

I want to thank Mr. Marcus Cowper from Ilios Publishing for getting this
project off the ground, and Nikolai Bogdanovic for editing this work.
Additionally, Giuseppe Rava created great artwork that significantly
contributes to the telling of the story of Leyte. My hat is off to him for this
superb effort. My colleagues in the U.S. Army War College's Department of
Distance Education deserve a great thank you for the support given to me
throughout this effort and for their encouragement. Finally, I could not
have completed this project without my family; their sacrifice allowed me
to finish my research and writing.

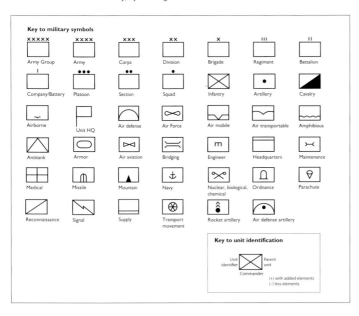

CONTENTS

ORIGINS OF THE CAMPAIGN   5

CHRONOLOGY   9

OPPOSING COMMANDERS   12
US commanders . Japanese commanders

OPPOSING FORCES   16
US forces . Japanese forces in the Philippines . Order of battle

OPPOSING PLANS   24
US plans . Japanese plans

THE CAMPAIGN   30
Initial moves . A-Day: October 20 . A-Day+1: On to Leyte Valley . The Battle of Leyte Gulf . Securing the Leyte Valley . Kenney's air power grounded . Securing the Ormoc Valley . Suzuki's last gamble: Burauen . From Deposito to Ormoc . The last stand: Palompon

AFTERMATH   88

THE BATTLEFIELD TODAY   93

FURTHER READING   94

INDEX   95

The approach to Leyte, July–October 1944.

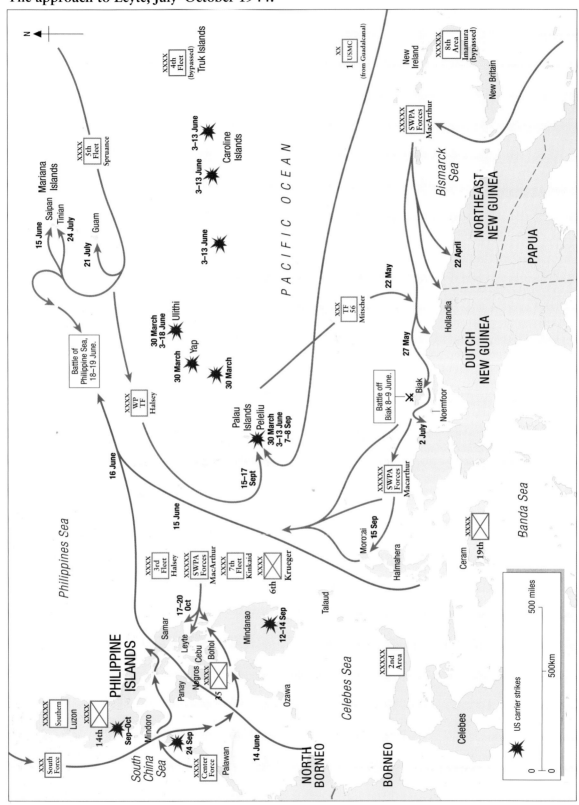

ORIGINS OF THE CAMPAIGN

In early 1942 the Japanese had rolled to victory throughout Asia and the Pacific. The United States, Australia, Great Britain, the Netherlands, China, and other powers feared that Japan would sweep away any opposition in their quest for expansion. At the time, the chance of mounting a major campaign against Tokyo seemed remote. However, by the summer of 1944 the strategic picture had changed in favor of the Allied Powers in all theaters. American and British forces had landed in Normandy. Italy was no longer wholly under Fascist control. The Soviet Union continued to push the Germans west. Moreover, Japan had suffered several major defeats.

Americans had put the Japanese on the strategic defensive. On March 24, 1942 the American–British Combined Chiefs of Staff (CCS) had agreed to allow Washington to determine Pacific war strategy. With this mandate, Washington responded. The US Navy (USN) had decimated the Imperial Japanese Navy (IJN) carrier forces at Midway in early June 1942. American submarines initiated a successful campaign against Japanese merchant ships. Army and Marine Corps forces had gone on the offensive at Guadalcanal, New Guinea, the Marshalls, and the Gilbert Islands. Japan was bogged down in China, which forced Tokyo to employ thousands of troops to pacify the country. By 1944, Washington was about to penetrate areas directly affecting Japan's survival. The Allies had successfully challenged the Japanese on the peripheral areas of their empire, but were now getting closer to Tokyo. Soon, the United States Army Air Forces (USAAF) would establish B-29 bomber bases that would deliver destruction directly over Honshu and Kyushu. Ground forces readied to strike in the Central Pacific and push north.

The only question for Washington centered on where American forces would initiate the main drive to defeat Japan. The American Joint Chiefs of Staff (JCS) had earlier agreed to focus on the Luzon, Formosa, and South China region to support bombing missions over Japan, cut off resource access, and prepare for a Japanese

MacArthur had suffered one of the US Army's greatest defeats in her history during the fight for the Philippines in 1942. The Japanese defeated a combined American and Filipino force that was numerically larger, but in some instances poorly trained and equipped. Here IJA forces celebrate in Bataan. MacArthur vowed to reverse this situation. The first step towards returning to the Philippines was retaking Leyte. (US Army)

home islands invasion. Before kicking off such a campaign, Washington needed to agree on a common strategy. In the Pacific, the Americans had two major lines of effort: the Central Pacific and the Southwest Pacific. The Central Pacific was under the control of Admiral Chester Nimitz and unsurprisingly featured a primarily naval focus and selected island-hopping to defeat or isolate the Japanese. In the Southwest Pacific, General Douglas MacArthur had driven up New Guinea towards the Philippines.

The JCS approached future Pacific strategy to defeat Japan under certain assumptions. With unconditional surrender as the agreed-upon Allied end state against the Axis Powers, Washington would have to conduct a campaign of primarily military means. This meant Allied forces would invade Japan to force its capitulation. For an invasion, JCS planners concluded that they needed a sustained bombing campaign to reduce Japanese military capabilities. Since the USAAF did not employ strategic bombers with sufficient range to hit Japan from Allied controlled areas in early 1944, the Americans required bases closer to Japan. One potential site was China, but logistical questions and the threat of territory loss to Japanese advances made this option untenable. Naval aviation could attack targets around Japan, but this required forward logistical and maintenance facilities. As MacArthur and Nimitz pushed north, plans to secure advanced bases developed. Additionally, to defeat Japan the Americans had to isolate Tokyo from her source of raw materials and food in Southeast Asia.

Two approaches developed. Admiral Ernest King, Chief of Naval Operations and Commander-in-Chief, United States Fleet, advocated an invasion of Formosa and the taking of Amoy, a Chinese port. King thought he could bypass the Philippines. This proposal allowed the United States to station B-29s and other aircraft closer to Japan to support aerial operations. Taking Formosa would create a large staging base to launch an invasion fleet against Japan, and would also block Japanese access to the South China Sea and Tokyo's shipments of oil, raw materials, and food from Southeast Asia. A further benefit was keeping China in the war. Although the Nationalist and Communist Chinese forces were fighting the Japanese in a grinding war of attrition, losses were still heavy among the scantily equipped, ill-trained, and poorly led Chinese soldiers. If China fell, the Japanese could transfer several divisions around the Pacific and make an invasion bloodier for Washington.

King believed a direct assault on Formosa was possible. His plan included bypassing all of the Philippine islands. In several approved plans (like JCS 713 "Strategy in the Pacific" dated February 16, 1944 and JCS/713/1 "Future Operations in the Pacific", dated March 10, 1944) the JCS agreed that

American soldiers, like these from the 7th Infantry Division, needed all of their training and experience, as well as the full range of available weaponry, to eject Japanese defenders throughout Leyte. Using fire and maneuver, US troops slowly advanced. Infantrymen had to use explosives, flamethrowers, and heavy artillery to push out the IJA. These soldiers would find the fighting in Leyte as tough as they did here on Kwajalein in early 1944. (US Army)

Formosa was the most important single objective in the China, Formosa, and Luzon areas. However, debate raged in Washington. Some critics believed that conducting such an operation required air and support facilities in the southern or central Philippine islands.

MacArthur disagreed about the plan to bypass the Philippines. Questions arose about the availability of sufficient naval forces to invade and sustain operations in Formosa and China. Skipping the Philippines would also leave significant Imperial Japanese Army (IJA) and IJN forces to do so and Allied lines. In addition, after

Washington had belittled Tokyo's pronouncements about creating the Greater East Asia Co-Prosperity Sphere and treatment of her occupied peoples, America would appear to have abandoned those same oppressed subjects in this move. Avoiding a fight in the Philippines could send the wrong message that Washington did not care about the Filipinos. Additionally, "abandoning" the Philippines would also prolong the deplorable treatment meted out to prisoners-of-war.

The counter-strategy to a Formosan campaign was to take the Philippines, ending with Luzon's conquest. Although this option would provoke heated debate among American strategic leaders, the emphasis on detouring all of the Philippines softened. Sending an invasion fleet against Formosa required Nimitz to support his campaign with naval aviation units alone. Land-based air forces did not have sufficient range from MacArthur's bases in the Southwest Pacific or Nimitz's current bases. Nimitz also needed a large land force to take Formosa. Building such a force required time. Supplying such an endeavor also involved a vast and complex system to feed, clothe, equip, and maintain this force. By March 1944, the JCS recognized the necessity for closer logistical and support bases if the Allies invaded Formosa. MacArthur received directions to plan an incursion into the southern Philippines.

Creating a base in the Philippines would enable Washington to continue planning to take Formosa or Luzon. While debate raged about selecting Formosa or Luzon, the Japanese were not idle. Tokyo also perceived the threat of further American moves in MacArthur's Southwest Pacific Area (SWPA) and Nimitz's Pacific Ocean Area (POA). The IJA and IJN, according to ULTRA cryptographic intercepts, started to strengthen their positions in Mindanao, Celebes, the Palau Islands, and other areas. To continue their move north, the Americans had to expand their front against the Japanese. Nimitz and MacArthur realized that capture of Leyte or Mindanao would improve operations. Nimitz's forces also made progress in the POA by capturing the Mariana Islands in June 1944. This was significant since the Americans now had B-29 bases to hit Japan, a key rationale for the Formosa option. Still, King did not abandon his plan to take Formosa. This came to a head when President Franklin Roosevelt, Nimitz, and MacArthur met on July 26, 1944 at Pearl Harbor. MacArthur and Nimitz debated both approaches. No official decision was made at the meeting, but Roosevelt was now thrust into the decision.

Leyte was the largest Pacific amphibious operation to date in the war. MacArthur used an all-army landing force in the campaign. The invading force was much greater than the IJA's defending forces, the 16th Division. The Americans were thankful that Suzuki had decided to not make a beachfront defense. Instead he would avoid massive pre-landing bombardments and plan on using counterattacks with reinforcements. (US Navy)

Meanwhile, Admiral William Halsey, Nimitz's Third Fleet commander, had already fought the Battle of the Philippine Sea, which severely weakened the remaining Japanese carrier forces. This allowed Halsey to conduct carrier strikes across the Philippines and prepare for actions against the Palau Islands. Halsey's planes had hit the Palau Islands on September 7–8, then Mindanao, and the central Philippines from September 12–14. MacArthur had already committed to taking Morotai, a stepping stone to the Philippines, on September 15.

Coincidentally, Halsey reported a limited Japanese military presence in the Central Philippines to Nimitz on September 12. The admiral identified that Leyte was "wide-open to attack" and advised taking it immediately. A downed USN pilot was informed by his Filipino rescuers that there was no Japanese presence on Leyte. MacArthur's staff knew otherwise since his headquarters had evidence of a significant enemy presence on Leyte. Halsey suggested canceling amphibious operations against Mindanao, Yap, the Palaus, and other sites. Nimitz radioed the JCS, who were with their British counterparts in Quebec during the Octagon Conference. Nimitz volunteered to provide naval and ground forces slated for Yap to MacArthur. General George Marshall, Chief of Staff of the Army, then contacted MacArthur's headquarters at Hollandia, New Guinea. Lieutenant-General Richard Sutherland, MacArthur's chief of staff, responded that MacArthur could take Leyte. MacArthur was at sea, with a Morotai invasion force, under radio silence. Sutherland disagreed with the suggestion of no Japanese on Leyte, but with Nimitz's additional forces, he believed MacArthur could overcome the IJA. The invasion date was set for October 20.

A key objective before the Leyte operation could commence was taking the island of Morotai. This island provided an air base for Kenney's aircraft to support future operations in the southern or central Philippines. Americans took the beaches on September 15, the same day as the attack on the Palau Islands. Eventually, heavy bombers, from Kenney's Thirteenth Air Force, flew from Morotai. (US Army)

Kenney used many different types of aircraft. The Consolidated B-24 Liberators allowed MacArthur's forces to hit targets at long range, given the proper basing, from New Guinea; Kenney sent B-24s to strike Davao in Mindanao. Unfortunately, Leyte was in the central Philippines and required MacArthur to take Morotai in order to base B-24s from the Thirteenth Air Force there. (US Air Force)

CHRONOLOGY

1941

December 8   Imperial Japanese forces attack the Philippines.

May 6   American and Filipino forces surrender unconditionally to the Japanese. Tokyo begins a long occupation of the Philippines.

1942

March 24   Anglo-American planners agree that the United States should lead the Pacific campaign planning for the Allies.

1943

February 25   MacArthur's SWPA staff initiate planning for recapturing the Philippines under the Reno plans series.

1944

March 10   The JCS approves proposals for future Pacific operations to include actions against Formosa for February 15, 1945.

June 13   The JCS requests comments by MacArthur and Nimitz on bypassing the Southern Philippines to invade Formosa or Japan.

July 4   Nimitz radios King's staff to suggest American forces acquire Mindanao as an air base for the Formosa operation.

July 9   Saipan falls; Tojo resigns as Japanese prime minister.

July 23   MacArthur releases schedule of SWPA future operations to include the capture of Morotai on September 15 and Mindanao on November 15.

July 24   Japanese Imperial General Headquarters (IGHQ) completes the *Sho-Go* series of plans to fight the decisive victory for the Pacific.

July 27   Roosevelt, MacArthur, and Nimitz meet at Pearl Harbor, Hawaii to discuss Pacific strategy. Questions arise about invading Formosa and leaving the Philippines untouched.

September 9   Halsey begins a carrier air strike campaign against Japanese targets in the Philippines, Formosa, and other locations.

September 12   Halsey reports that Leyte is unoccupied and suggests American forces invade the island. The JCS queries MacArthur's staff about a Leyte invasion. Sutherland replies that an invasion is feasible and the invasion date is set for October 20.

September 15	American forces invade Morotai. Halsey's Western Pacific Task Force invades the Palaus.
September 21	GHQ SWPA releases Operations Instruction 70 outlining the invasion of Leyte. MacArthur also reports to the JCS that he can land on Luzon by December 20; he suggests a Formosa invasion is unnecessary.
October 10	General Yamashita Tomoyuki takes command of the Fourteenth Area Army in Manila.
October 13	VII Amphibious Force sails from Hollandia to Leyte.
October 14	III Amphibious Force at Manus departs for Leyte
October 17	Elements of the 6th Ranger Battalion take Suluan and Dingat islands in Leyte Gulf. The Americans begin minesweeping operations in routes into and around the invasion sites. Japanese radio stations receive word of the American landings. The IJN Combined Fleet commander and the IJA headquarters initiate *Sho-Go 1*.
October 18	Delayed by a day, US Rangers take Homonhon Island. Seventh Fleet ships bombard Leyte's beaches.
October 19	All American invasion convoys converge into Leyte Gulf.
October 20	The Sixth Army invades Leyte. Operations concentrate near Tacloban, Dulag, and the Panaon Strait. Admiral Soemu Toyoda orders IJN forces to destroy Kinkaid's invasion force in Leyte Gulf.
October 21	American forces near Dulag face determined Japanese opposition. The 1st US Cavalry Division enters Tacloban.
October 22	Terauchi decides to organize his forces for a tough fight on Leyte to destroy the American invaders. Krueger's forces consolidate positions near Dulag and start to push out the Japanese defenders.
October 23	MacArthur restores the Philippine Civil Government. Cavalrymen from the 1st US Cavalry Division start moving north on land and through amphibious operations to control the San Juanico Strait. Supply issues arise for the Americans.
October 24	American forces push inland. The next few days see Krueger taking Burauen and nearby airfields. Japanese reinforcement convoys from Luzon start under Operation *TA*.
October 25	Start of the Battle of Leyte Gulf. Kinkaid's ships survive Japanese naval attacks. Japanese land forces continue to resist the Americans, especially in the XXIV Corps area, but start to give ground under pressure.
October 27	Kenney sends P-38s from the 475th Fighter Group to Tacloban.

October 29	The 24th Infantry Division seizes Jaro. 96th Infantry Division finally clears Catmon Hill. American units move out towards Abuyog and Baybay.
October 30	Japanese forces stop the 24th Infantry Division efforts to move north from Jaro to Carigara. The 7th Infantry Division seizes Baybay.
November 1	IJA 1st Division elements land at Ormoc
November 2	Krueger clears out the Leyte Valley, Carigara falls into American hands.
November 6	US X Corps units probe Breakneck Ridge. This action starts efforts to move south on Highway 2 to Ormoc. The Americans will eventually break through only after Krueger's men move north from Ormoc weeks later. XXIV Corps tries to move west of Dagami.
November 8–9	Fifth Air Force and USN forces attack Japanese convoys attempting to land at Ormoc. The Battle of Ormoc Bay results in major losses to transports and IJA reinforcements to *TA-3* and *TA-4* convoys.
November 14	Krueger continues efforts to clear Breakneck Ridge. 7th Infantry Division begins its push from Damulaan towards Ormoc.
November 22	32nd Infantry Division captures Limon and finally completes the fight for Breakneck Ridge.
November 23	Japanese forces attack 7th Infantry Division at Shoestring Ridge.
November 27	Kaoru Raiding Detachment fails to accomplish any significant damage to Burauen airfields.
December 5	Krueger launches an amphibious operation to bypass Japanese positions near the Palanas River and nearby ridges.
December 6	IJA 16th Division soldiers start the *Wa* operation that will ultimately fail. Japanese paratroopers drop on Buri and San Pablo airfields.
December 7	77th Infantry Division lands south of Deposito.
December 10	Ormoc falls to American soldiers.
December 18	77th Infantry Division units seize Valencia airfield.
December 21	X and XXIV Corps units meet on Highway 2. The Americans essentially control the Ormoc Valley.
December 25	MacArthur announces the end of major combat operations on Leyte.
December 26	The US Eighth Army replaces the Sixth Army on Leyte. Mopping-up operations continue until May 1945.

OPPOSING COMMANDERS

US COMMANDERS

The Allied forces, consisting almost exclusively of Americans, in Leyte had one dominating personality, **General Douglas MacArthur**. As the Supreme Commander, SWPA, he had a strong Philippines connection. Born on January 26, 1880 and the son of Lieutenant-General and Congressional Medal of Honor (CMH) winner Arthur MacArthur, Jr, Douglas MacArthur was in command of US Army Forces in the Far East (USAFFE) in Manila before the war. He survived the successful Japanese 1941–42 campaign against the Philippines; President Roosevelt had ordered him to evacuate to Australia and take command of SWPA.

Graduating first in his class at the US Military Academy (USMA) in 1903, his first overseas assignment was to the Philippines where he conducted surveys to include Tacloban City, Leyte. MacArthur demonstrated personal bravery and initiative throughout his career. During the 1914 Veracruz Expedition, his commander had recommended him for the CMH, but the award escaped him. MacArthur's superiors nominated him for the CMH after the Meuse-Argonne Offensive in World War I. The Army disapproved it. After the war, MacArthur served as the USMA Superintendent, Commanding General Department of the Philippines, and Army Chief of Staff. After retiring from the Army, MacArthur accepted an appointment as a field marshal in the burgeoning Philippine Army. Roosevelt recalled MacArthur to active duty to command the USAFFE. Awarded the CMH for the Philippines defense, MacArthur subsequently led a successful campaign across the Southwest Pacific.

MacArthur steadfastly lobbied Washington to devote more attention and resources to the Pacific against the Japanese. He helped sway the Joint Chiefs of Staff to maintain a two-pronged strategy against the Japanese empire through the SWPA and Central Pacific. His focus on liberating the Philippines would later pit him against the US Navy's efforts to advance to Formosa and avoid recapturing Luzon in 1944. He later succeeded in directing American forces against Luzon.

General Douglas MacArthur was commander SWPA who oversaw the Allied effort to conquer Leyte. He had already completed a full US Army career, but was recalled to active duty. During the war, he had stormy relationships with Washington, the US Navy, and members of his own staff. He was uncompromising about his desire to return to the Philippines. (National Archives)

Washington named MacArthur as the commander of US Army Forces Pacific in preparation for the invasion of Japan. With Tokyo's surrender, MacArthur then became Supreme Commander for the Allied Powers in Japan. MacArthur took on the daunting challenge of constructing major political, economic, and social changes in postwar Japan.

Lieutenant General Walter Krueger served as the commander of MacArthur's Sixth Army. He emigrated from Flatow, West Prussia, as a child, to the United States. The future general left high school in 1898 to enlist in the Army to fight in the Spanish American War of 1898. He sailed for Cuba and later fought in the Philippines against Emilio Aguinaldo's insurgents, where he earned a commission in 1901. Krueger also served during the Mexican Punitive Expedition in 1916 and he deployed to France during World War I.

After World War I, Krueger's reputation as a top instructor and trainer was established. The Army sent him to the Infantry School at Fort Benning, Georgia, and he later commanded the 55th Infantry Regiment, which cemented his ties to the infantry. Krueger also attended and later served as an instructor at both the Army and Naval war colleges. The future Sixth Army commander served twice in the Army War Plans Division and successfully commanded at brigade, divisional, and corps levels.

World War II brought Krueger great fame. On December 7, 1941, Krueger led the Third Army and Southern Defense Command. He became the initial commander of the Sixth Army and oversaw its deployment to Australia in January 1943. Under MacArthur, the Sixth Army fought in a number of campaigns in the SWPA. Krueger saw action in Kiriwina and the Woodlock Islands, New Britain, the Admiralty Islands, New Guinea, Morotai, and Leyte. Krueger would later participate in the invasions of Mindoro and Luzon. The Sixth Army fought a bitter contest against Japanese defenders in Manila and in northern Luzon. MacArthur brought Krueger to Japan for occupation duty, and he retired in 1946.

Lieutenant-General George Kenney changed the face of land-based air power in the Pacific. His first service came as a pilot in the 91st Aero Squadron in France during World War I, where the Army credited him with two aircraft kills. He became a key proponent of making the Air Corps independent from the Army. Kenney joined MacArthur's staff in March 1942. He directed the Allied Air Forces and Fifth Air Force in the SWPA. Kenney modified medium bombers by adding machine guns and cannons for use against Japanese shipping, introduced skip-bombing, and changed supply techniques to improve aerial deliveries, among other innovations. In an era where American air commanders focused on strategic bombing, Kenney greatly improved MacArthur's combat operations through tactical air capabilities. After the war, Kenney became the Air Force's first commander of the nuclear-armed Strategic Air Command.

Walter Krueger, right, shown as a general, commanded the Sixth Army on Leyte with success. However, MacArthur criticized him for the slow advance through the island. Krueger never finished high school, but advanced rapidly up the career ladder in the US Army. He would later lead the Sixth Army in the campaign for Luzon. (US Army)

Admiral Thomas Kinkaid took command of MacArthur's naval forces. Kinkaid graduated from the US Naval Academy in 1908. Kinkaid trained as a gunnery officer onboard the USS *Arizona* during World War I. After the war, the Navy assigned him to Turkey. He later commanded a destroyer and cruiser, became a staff officer, and served as an attaché in Italy and Yugoslavia. Kinkaid advanced to command Cruiser Division 6 in November 1941 for the Pacific Fleet.

During the Pacific War, Kinkaid participated in campaigns against Rabaul and New Guinea, in the Coral Sea, at Midway, in the Eastern Solomons and Santa Cruz Islands, and on Guadalcanal. He led the efforts to recapture the Aleutian Islands. Kinkaid subsequently moved to the SWPA as MacArthur's commander for the Allied Naval Forces and US Seventh Fleet. He executed amphibious operations throughout New Guinea, Leyte, and Luzon, and would go on to fight at Leyte Gulf, the last major battleship engagement of the war. Kinkaid's surface fleet held off the Japanese at the Surigao Strait. After the war, he commanded the Sixteenth Fleet before retiring in the postwar demobilization.

George C. Kenney, then a lieutenant-general, served MacArthur as his Allied Air Forces commander. MacArthur had fired previous air commanders, but Kenney's success and ability to cut the "dead wood" from his organization made MacArthur a firm supporter of him. Kenney successfully introduced innovative tactics, new munitions, modified aircraft, and integrated the air forces with land forces to great effect in the SWPA. (US Air Force)

Vice Admiral William F Halsey, Jr led the Third Fleet under Nimitz. He graduated from the US Naval Academy in 1904. Halsey served initially in the Navy's surface fleet and was an attaché in Berlin. Halsey made a calculated career change when he qualified as an aviation observer. This allowed him to command the aircraft carrier USS *Saratoga* and later take charge of carrier division units. Halsey was at Pearl Harbor on the eve of war, but was at sea on his flagship, the USS *Enterprise*, during the attack on Hawaii. He later commanded the Doolittle Raid carrier force, fought in the South Pacific, at the Palaus, at Leyte Gulf, and on Luzon. He retired as a fleet admiral.

JAPANESE COMMANDERS

General Count Terauchi Hisaichi, the IJA's Southern Army commander, governed the Southeast Asia region, including the Philippines, for Tokyo. Son of a former prime minister, Terauchi received his baptism of fire during the Russo-Japanese War in February 1904. He served as an attaché in Vienna, then held several unit commands, before eventually rising to become Army War Minister. As commander of the Southern Army, he and Admiral Yamamoto Isoroku planned the conquest of Malaya, the Philippines, and the Netherlands East Indies.

Terauchi had initially believed the main American attack in the Philippines would be directed against Luzon. He would later clash with subordinates over the *Sho-Go* order to reinforce Leyte, at the expense of defending Luzon, for the decisive battle for the island. Terauchi later surrendered the Southern Army to Lord Louis Mountbatten, and died of a brain hemorrhage in Malaya in 1946.

General Yamashita Tomoyuki took charge of the Fourteenth Area Army on October 10, 1944 with the mission to defend the Philippines. Yamashita's first taste of combat occurred in 1914 fighting against the Germans in China.

He would later be assigned as an attaché in Berlin, Bern, and Vienna. Yamashita joined a political movement that rivaled that of the future Japanese leader Tojo Hideki, who had Yamashita transferred to a command in China to neutralize his influence in the movement. Tokyo did rescue him before the outbreak of war by making him the Twenty-Fifth Army commander. This command would lead the IJA in Malaya. Here, he defeated the British Commonwealth forces and captured Singapore. With this honor, Yamashita became the "Tiger of Malaya." Tojo sidelined him once again after this victory with a reassignment to China.

General Yamashita Tomoyuki replaced Lieutenant-General Kuroda Shigenori as the Fourteenth Area Army commander on the eve of the Leyte invasion, on October 9, 1944. Yamashita had little time to prepare the Philippines for an American invasion. He disagreed with his superior commanders on their emphasis to defend Leyte at the expense of Luzon. At the end of the war, he was tried as a war criminal and executed after a controversial trial. (US Army)

After the Americans took Saipan, Tojo's government fell and the replacement government in Tokyo reassigned Yamashita to the Fourteenth Area Army. Despite the American victory and fall of Manila on Luzon, he continued to resist the Americans on Luzon until his surrender on September 2, 1945. MacArthur later brought him to trial as a war criminal for Japanese actions during the recapture of Manila. During the controversial trial, the jury found Yamashita guilty. American forces executed him on February 23, 1946.

Yamashita relied on **Lieutenant-General Suzuki Sosaku** to conduct the primary ground defense of Leyte. Suzuki's military career included a tour in Germany, as a staff officer in the Kwantung Army plus other additional staff assignments, and as chief of staff for the Central China Expeditionary Force. He also served as Yamashita's chief of staff for the Twenty-Fifth Army in Malaya. Suzuki held a series of transportation commands until named as the Thirty-Fifth Army commander responsible for Leyte. He survived the fighting on Leyte, only to die attempting to escape capture on Mindanao on April 19, 1945.

Japanese commanders faced many problems in the field during the Leyte campaign. Poor weather, isolated units, and jungle terrain all contributed to limited communications particularly between parent and subordinate units, which affected command and control of operations. This would later degrade IJA activities including the Burauen effort to capture several American-held airfields. (US Army)

OPPOSING FORCES

US FORCES

The American forces assigned to eject the IJA and IJN from Leyte came from MacArthur's SWPA command and units temporarily reassigned from Nimitz's POA command. Since some of MacArthur's SWPA ground forces could not disengage for the Leyte invasion, Nimitz had offered MacArthur two divisions for the initial island landings. MacArthur required help from Nimitz to support his naval forces. Nimitz's carriers had conducted raids across Formosa to the Philippines to reduce Imperial Japanese Navy Air Forces (IJNAF) and Imperial Japanese Army Air Forces (IJAAF) that threatened MacArthur's operation, and they disrupted enemy positions ahead of the Leyte invasion. MacArthur's naval forces provided some amphibious landing capabilities. Air power was another key force. Carrier aviation, from Nimitz and the SWPA's Task Force (TF) 77, provided the initial air support for MacArthur's ground operations until Kenney's Fifth Air Force could establish air bases on Leyte.

A huge advantage that Krueger could bring to bear on Leyte was armor. However, Leyte had few roads for tanks to exploit. Leyte did offer large areas to maneuver, but frequently that terrain consisted of jungles, mountains, swamps, rivers, and other obstacles that slowed American advances despite the advantage in medium tanks like this M-4 Sherman. (US Army)

MacArthur's main ground assault force against Leyte was the Sixth Army under Krueger. Sixth Army contained two corps: the X and XXIV (from Nimitz). Major-General Franklin Sibert led X Corps with the 1st Cavalry Division and 24th Infantry Division. Major-General John Hodge controlled the XXIV Corps' 7th and 96th Infantry divisions. Krueger also had the 21st Regimental Combat Team (RCT) and the 6th Ranger Battalion. MacArthur could deploy his Sixth Army Reserve with the 32nd and 77th Infantry divisions plus the 381st RCT if the main assault force faced unexpected resistance. The Army Service Command (ASC) supplied engineering and general logistical support. ASC activities became an essential element for the Allies for road and airfield construction. Additionally, ground and air commanders required a vast amount of rations, ammunition, spare parts, and weapons. Without them, MacArthur's offensive might falter. MacArthur counted on 202,500 troops for the invasion. X Corps forces consisted of about

Landing on Pacific islands required unique capabilities. Unlike the European, Mediterranean, and North African amphibious operations, Pacific assaults required which [illegible] Shown is a LVT unit that allowed US Army and USMC units more protection against Japanese fire while they negotiated an assault. These Water Buffalos could carry troops or provide fire support. (US Coast Guard)

53,000 men while the XXIV Corps mustered 51,000. Krueger initially deployed 174,000 combat and support personnel for the initial assault.

MacArthur's X Corps, composed of combat veterans, had succeeded in pushing the Japanese west in New Guinea and to the Admiralties. The XXIV Corps had only one division with combat experience, the 7th Infantry, which had served in the Aleutian Islands before its transfer to fight in the tropics. The 96th Infantry Division would cut its teeth in combat for the first time during the Leyte operation.

The Sixth Army relied heavily upon firepower. Notably, fire support through field artillery helped break up Japanese positions and allowed the Americans to advance. Fire and maneuver let American ground forces avoid head-on attacks, which reduced casualties. The reliance on this also required extensive supply support, which could slow the offensive if the Japanese contested any American movements, especially at night.

American firepower required massive munitions supply. MacArthur's forces had the luxury, at this point of the war, of a peaking war economy. Despite a two-front Pacific and European conflict, MacArthur could count on vast materiel to fight with. However, limited shipping, distribution, and changes to planning affected the logistics in the Leyte operation.

Another force that MacArthur could call upon was the Filipino guerillas. Active since the fall of the Philippines, they consisted of former Philippine Army soldiers, escaped Americans, disaffected Filipino civilians, and others. Japanese occupying forces had relied on a docile Filipino population to avoid large, garrison-bound forces to pacify the islands. The Japanese occupation was troubled. For example, the need for increased Philippine food imports, to fill empty warehouses in Japan due in part to an American submarine blockade, caused Filipino hunger and unrest. An insurgency movement grew. IJA forces remained in garrison to protect cities, and the absence of Japanese or Filipino labor slowed the construction of airfields and

American soldiers had a relative advantage with mobility. Their edge over the Japanese with vehicles allowed Krueger to rapidly deploy forces and conduct maneuvers to support operations faster than Suzuki. Here an M-29 Weasel cargo carrier moves past a Filipino town. The Weasel was amphibious and could operate in swampy areas around Leyte. (US Army)

defensive positions. Japanese officers estimated in the spring of 1944 that between 200,000 and 300,000 Filipino guerillas operated in ten sectors. The guerillas reported all types of information regarding Japanese positions, movements, strengths, and other data through at least 50 radio stations to the Allies. Insurgents also conducted sabotage, attacked rear areas, provided reconnaissance, and conducted combat operations when the Americans arrived.

MacArthur had his own naval forces under Kinkaid's Seventh Fleet. Kinkaid commanded the central Philippines attack force TF-77, which oversaw two other task forces: TF-78 supported the northern beach assault on San Jose, while TF-79 landed forces on the southern beaches near Dulag. Kinkaid also had seven task group (TG) subordinate commands composed of TG-77.1 Flagship Group, TG-77.2 Fire Support Group, TG-77.3 Close Covering Group, TG-77.4 Escort Carrier Group, TG-77.5 Minesweeping and Hydrographic Group, TG-77.6 Beach Demolition Group, and TG-77.7 Service Group. TF-78 would move from Hollandia with the 24th Infantry Division and ASC to Leyte. The 1st Cavalry Division readied itself at Manus. TF-79, formerly TF-33, also supported Leyte operations after the cancellation of the Yap invasion. TF-79 deployed from Hawaii. Kinkaid's amphibious fleet alone had over 520 ships with 420 transports.

Supporting Kinkaid was Nimitz's Third Fleet, under Admiral William Halsey, which made up one of the largest combined naval forces in the Pacific up to this time. The Third and Seventh fleets had a combined strength of 32 carriers. Halsey controlled the powerful TF-38, with fast carriers, consisting of 15 flattops with 925 aircraft. MacArthur could deploy 12 battleships to provide significant direct fire support against IJA beach defenses or potentially fend off attacks by Japanese surface ships. Kinkaid and Halsey could also call on 23 cruisers and 100 destroyers to screen the fleet, direct fire onto the landing areas, and provide anti-aircraft (AA) fire. American submariners also patrolled the waters throughout the region. They gathered information on Japanese movements and provided valuable attack capability against the IJN. If Halsey's naval forces required resupply or refitting, they would need to sail to Ulithi in the Western Caroline Islands.

Halsey's Third Fleet was responsible for protecting Kinkaid's Seventh Fleet from an IJN attack. However, there were some command and control issues. Although nominally assigned to MacArthur, Halsey also received guidance from Nimitz to reduce the Imperial Japanese air and naval forces in the Philippines, on Formosa, the Ryukyu Islands, and other targets that did not appear to have a direct bearing on Leyte. The reduction in air forces on Luzon, Formosa, and other Philippine islands did help weaken available IJAAF and IJNAF forces to strike the Sixth Army and Third Fleet on Leyte. Although Halsey's assignment involved support to MacArthur, Nimitz worried about the remaining IJN Combined Fleet. Nimitz directed Halsey to

American forces for the initial Leyte operation came from a variety of sources. MacArthur assigned SWPA divisions while Nimitz contributed two divisions to the effort. These troops are preparing to board transports in the Admiralties Islands for the October 20 landings on Leyte. The soldiers in this photograph are probably from the 1st Cavalry Division that boarded transports on Manus Island. (US Army)

seek and destroy the Japanese fleet if the opportunity arose. This directive conflicted with the objective of providing direct support for the Leyte invasion and created the conditions where the IJN had an opportunity to exploit differences between Halsey and Kinkaid's forces. These differences highlighted issues of unity of command for the Americans in terms of critical naval support, especially for air forces early in the campaign.

George Kenney's Allied Air Forces commanded a number of capabilities that would support MacArthur's forces on Leyte, should they be able to operate

TG-38.3 served as a strike force that hit the Philippines and other targets with carrier aircraft. Halsey's planes were vital for MacArthur in providing air support early in the campaign. However, Halsey redirected his forces to search for IJN carriers. They also needed to return to Ulithi to refit the fleet; where these ships are headed after operations against the Japanese. Both actions created a gap for the American air effort. (US Navy)

from the island. Once the Sixth Army's engineers prepared the airfields near Tacloban, Burauen, and Dulag, Kenney could fully deploy the Fifth Air Force. Meanwhile, other Allied Air Forces elements would respond to any threats on the western flanks and rear of MacArthur's advance north. Halsey's Third Fleet carriers covered operations east of Leyte. They would act to isolate Japanese forces from Leyte. Kenney also directed aircraft from the Royal Australian Air Force (RAAF), Northern Solomons Command (composed of Marine Corps and Royal New Zealand air units with about 530 aircraft) and Far East Air Forces (FEAF). RAAF personnel and aircraft replaced Fifth Air Force units in New Guinea and other locations south of Leyte. FEAF had two major air forces, the Fifth and Thirteenth. Overall, Kenney commanded 2,800 aircraft throughout the SWPA on October 17, 1944, many of which were destined for the Philippines.

Fifth Air Force's commander, Major-General Ennis Whitehead, would conduct most of Kenney's Leyte operations. Whitehead used his 38th Bomb Group's B-24s to hit targets from captured territory like Morotai. Kenney's first objective was to send his 8th Fighter Group's P-38 aircraft to gain air superiority and intercept convoys, among other tasks. With Kenney's air

American forces used a number of vehicles throughout the Leyte campaign. Amphibious tracked vehicles (like this LVT A-4) helped bring troops ashore, carried supplies over streams and tough terrain, and they could support attacks from land or sea. The LVT A-4 had a 75mm howitzer that could deliver high-explosive and other munitions against Japanese defenders. The US Army and USMC used these vehicles extensively throughout the Pacific. (US Army)

control, aircraft such as medium bombers could operate from Leyte. Additionally, once the Fifth Air Force deployed on Leyte, the Thirteenth could move onto the island. Before MacArthur started the campaign, Kenney's units embarked on an aircraft replacement program. Whitehead received B-25J and H models modified to deliver heavier firepower against surface targets. FEAF pilots also operated A-20G Havocs, P-47s, and P-40s that could hit ground targets. Kenney's aircraft maintenance crews modified aircraft with external and internal fuel tanks to extend their ranges to those now required. Fifth Air Force had 1,100 operational aircraft out of 1,320 planes with 230 medium and heavy bombers. The Thirteenth Air Force counted on 275 operational aircraft, with 170 bombers, to mount sorties. Kenney had sufficient land-based air forces for Leyte, but they awaited adequate airfields from which to operate.

One of the keys to SWPA GHQ success was its air power. As B-25s increased their presence on Leyte, they were able to support interdiction and other missions. Extra firepower in more maneuverable aircraft like the B-25 or A-20 added an extra punch. Some of these planes carried one 75mm cannon that could fire off three shots while covering a 1,500-yard (1,370m) approach. (US Air Force)

In the initial operations, MacArthur relied on naval aviation. This was not a permanent solution. The Third and Seventh Fleet carrier aviation had to operate on limited fuel and munitions stores at sea. This constrained their operating capability and they would eventually need to resupply. MacArthur could also call upon Nimitz's land-based POA aircraft if there were problems; this included about 110 B-24s. If Japanese forces tried to deliver reinforcements from the southern Chinese coast, Nineteenth Air Force aircraft could respond against Japanese ports or convoys. Similarly, Kenney had the option to use Twentieth Air Force's B-29s to support the Leyte operation by bombing possible reinforcements in the form of Formosa-based Japanese forces.

Major Fifth Air Force units assigned to Leyte, October–December 1944

Moving Kenney's Fifth Air Force units to Leyte was mired in the lack of suitable air base capacity early in the campaign. As the campaign unfolded and engineers expanded air bases, Kenney moved operational units to Leyte. Kenney sent fighter units first to establish air superiority, then bombers. Other units arrived later, but by this time major operations had already moved to Luzon.

Units	Aircraft	Location	Date arrived
49th Fighter Group	P-38J/L	Tacloban	October 24, 1944
421st Night Fighter Squadron	P-61	Tacloban	October 25, 1944
475th Fighter Group	P-38J/L	Dulag	October 28, 1944
22nd Bombardment Group	B-24, B-25	Dulag	November 15, 1944
43rd Bombardment Group	B-24	Tacloban	November 15, 1944
348th Fighter Group	P-47	Tacloban	November 16, 1944
3rd Bombardment Group	A-20, B-25	Dulag	November 16, 1944
312th Bombardment Group	B-25	Tacloban	November 19, 1944
345th Bombardment Group	B-25	Dulag	November 1944
417th Bombardment Group	A-20	Tacloban	December 6, 1944
3rd Air Commando Group	Various	Various	December 1944

JAPANESE FORCES IN THE PHILIPPINES

Tokyo faced an unenviable strategic situation in October 1944. Nimitz's forces had moved through the Marianas and threatened to strike Formosa, the Ryukyu Islands, Iwo Jima, or even the Japanese home islands. MacArthur had moved through New Guinea and now appeared poised to return to the Philippines. Positioning forces along all possible avenues of Allied advance was infeasible for Tokyo. IGHQ planners responded with the *Sho Go* plans, which would send maximum resources to meet the first location of major Allied action. Both Terauchi and Yamashita considered that their Philippine forces anchored Southeast Asia's defense. Terauchi recognized the importance of the Philippines and had relocated the Southern Army's headquarters from Singapore to Manila in May 1944. The Southern Army controlled forces located from Burma to New Guinea, to include the Philippines.

Washington and SWPA intelligence officers disagreed about the IJA strength in the Philippines. By October 3, War Department officials, using decrypted Japanese diplomatic messages, distributed under the codename MAGIC and covered by the secretive Allied ULTRA program, believed that Tokyo had assigned about 225,000 troops throughout the Philippines. SWPA officials estimated it was higher at 242,000 men. GHQ SWPA projected IJA Philippine forces had grown from 191,500 in July to 224,000 at the end of September. Intelligence officers also noticed increased aircraft deployments to the Philippines. Clearly, the Japanese had accepted that the probability was high that the Americans' next move was the Philippines. As early as June, IGHQ officers ordered the Fourteenth Area Army to convert four independent mixed brigades into divisions using replacements to fill out these new units. Japanese units throughout the Philippines could offer a large pool of reinforcements to oppose wherever MacArthur set foot on the islands.

MacArthur's main foe in Leyte was Suzuki's Thirty-Fifth Army based in the Visayan Islands. Suzuki directed several divisions (1st, 16th, 26th, 102nd, and elements of the 30th), plus three independent mixed brigades (54th, 55th, and 68th). He assigned Lieutenant-General Makino Shiro's 16th Division to defend Leyte near Dulag. Makino concentrated much of his division near Dulag since he anticipated MacArthur's amphibious forces would land on the southern beaches of eastern Leyte. Curiously, Makino did not assign many forces to defend Tacloban, Leyte's largest city, nor the island's west coast. He established his headquarters north of Tacloban in a "rear" area. The IJN had deployed a naval garrison and construction units on the island.

Another important IJA force in the Philippines was the Fourth Air Army. This IJAAF organization, based in Manila, was responsible for the Philippines air defense. Under Japanese Battle Preparations No. 11, March 1944, the air forces (both IJAAF and IJNAF) had the initial responsibility of defending the Philippines. Air forces could strike the Allies over broad distances without having to base themselves at a specific location. The IJAAF's Fourth Air Army, under Lieutenant-General Tominaga Kyoji, had received reinforcements from the Second Air Army in Manchuria. The 2nd Air Division

Americans were not the only ones fighting in poor weather and with inadequate transportation on Leyte. Here a Japanese depiction of a supply transport unit slogging along narrow trails that have been turned into a muddy mess shows the conditions both sides had to endure. Slow transportation of supplies, rations, and replacements translated into weakened combat capability for Suzuki. (US Army)

controlled the majority of aircraft defending the Philippines with reinforcements from China, Formosa, and Japan. However, IJAAF losses continued to plague Tokyo in New Guinea and other areas that had their own defensive responsibilities. Still, the Fourth Air Army received reinforcements from Malaya, the Celebes, and North Borneo.

The 2nd Air Division deployed its forces throughout the Philippines, but with no significant forces on Leyte. Tominaga assigned heavy and light bombers on the former FEAF Clark Field site. IJAAF pilots flew fighters from the Manila area and bombers from Lipa. Tominaga also moved fighters and reconnaissance units to Baclod, in the Negros, for possible action in the central or southern Philippines. These moves allowed aircraft to have sufficient range to operate over Leyte. Before MacArthur set foot on Leyte, Halsey's fast carriers had struck the Philippines, resulting in the IJAAF and IJNAF suffering large aircraft losses. Washington, using MAGIC and other ULTRA-level decrypted messages, estimated that the Fourth Air Army had lost over 200 airplanes in these attacks,

One of the problems Yamashita and Suzuki faced in Leyte was a lack of time. Although there were Japanese forces in the Philippines, they did not have sufficient time to complete adequate defenses to fend off the Americans. Filipino guerillas, a hostile occupied populace, limited resources, and other issues hampered the Japanese from the start of the *Sho-Go* operation. (US Army)

reducing the IJAAF, on the archipelago, to about 225 planes. The Fourth Air Army actually had 104 operating aircraft out of 194 remaining fighters, bombers, reconnaissance, and other types to counter an American assault.

IJNAF land-based aircraft comprised the other main air forces that would contest American ground operations on Leyte. Nimitz's Pacific Fleet had already destroyed most of the IJN's carrier fleet and aircraft. Still, the IJNAF could field the First and Second Air fleets over the Philippines. Training units, replacements, remaining carrier aircraft, and other Japan-based squadrons replaced combat losses in the summer of 1944. The First Air Fleet deployed to Luzon, at Clark Field. The air fleet's Fifth Base Air Force supplied the primary IJNAF forces facing MacArthur. By September 1, the Fifth Base Air Force had only 250 operational aircraft out of a 410-plane force. Continued American carrier strikes, maintenance issues, and the arrival of reinforcements made accurate strength estimates difficult. Still, IJNAF pilots flew long reconnaissance missions to detect any American naval movements that might indicate where they would invade. By October 10, American intelligence officers calculated that the Japanese could fly 203 IJNAF aircraft of which

As the Americans gathered their invasion fleet in Leyte Gulf, Vice Admiral Onishi Takijiro, First Air Fleet commander, formed a suicide strike force in Manila composed of 24 volunteers from the 201st (Fighter) Attack Group. Onishi's kamikaze Special Attack Corps first took flight on October 21, but did not hit any American ships. The kamikaze concept would prove more deadly later in the war. (US Army)

115 were fighters. The Second Air Fleet remained in Kyushu, but could transfer reinforcements to Manila from its 737 aircraft inventory. The IJNAF also provided another deadly air weapon: kamikaze suicide planes.

IJN surface fleets supported Japanese ground forces on Leyte mostly through transport of reinforcements and resupply. The IJN's Combined Fleet would attempt to destroy Halsey's fleet and the amphibious forces in a decisive battle at sea, but it would fail in the Battle of Leyte Gulf.

ORDER OF BATTLE

US FORCES: SWPA ORGANIZATION FOR LEYTE

GENERAL HEADQUARTERS, SOUTHWEST PACIFIC AREA (GENERAL DOUGLAS MACARTHUR)
Sixth Army (Lieutenant-General Walter Krueger)
X Corps (Major-General Franklin Sibert)
  1st Cavalry Division
  24th Infantry Division
XXIV Corps (Major-General John Hodge)
  7th Infantry Division
  96th Infantry Division
  20th Armored Group
  503rd Parachute Infantry Regiment
  11th Airborne Division
Sixth Army Reserve
  32nd Infantry Division
  77th Infantry Division
  381st Regimental Combat Team (part of the 96th Infantry Division)
Army Service Command
Independent Sixth Army units
  2nd Engineer Support Brigade
  6th Ranger Battalion
  21st Regimental Combat Team (part of the 24th Infantry Division)
Eighth Army (Lieutenant-General Robert L. Eichelberger) (reinforcement to Sixth Army)
Allied Air Forces (Lieutenant-General George Kenney)
Fifth Air Force
Thirteenth Air Force
Allied Naval Forces, Seventh Fleet (Vice Admiral Thomas C. Kinkaid)
Northern Attack Force, Task Force 78 (VII Amphibious Force)
Task Group 78.1 Palo Attack Group
Task Group 78.2 San Ricardo Attack Group
Task Group 78.3 Panaon Attack Group
Task Group 78.4 Dingat Attack Group
Task Group 78.5 Harbor Entrance Control Group
Task Group 78.6 Reinforcement Group 1
Task Group 78.7 Reinforcement Group 2
Task Group 78.8 Reinforcement Group 3
Southern Attack Force, Task Force 79 (III Amphibious Force)
Task Group 79.1 Attack Group A
Task Group 79.2 Attack Group B
Task Group 79.3 Transport Group A
Task Group 79.4 Transport Group B
Task Group 79.11 Screen
US Army Services of Supply
Third Fleet (Admiral William F. Halsey, Jr); attached to MacArthur from Nimitz

IJA FORCES AVAILABLE FOR LEYTE

SOUTHERN ARMY (FIELD MARSHAL TERAUCHI HISACHI)
Fourteenth Area Army (General Yamashita Tomoyuki)
Thirty-Fifth Army (Lieutenant-General Suzuki Sosaku)
  1st Division
  16th Division
  26th Division
  102nd Division
  Elements of 30th Division
  54th Independent Mixed Brigade
  55th Independent Mixed Brigade
  68th Independent Mixed Brigade
Fourth Air Army (Lieutenant-General Tominaga Kyōji)
2nd Air Division
4th Air Division
3rd Shipping Transport Command (Major-General Inada Masazumi)

JAPANESE GROUND FORCES ON LEYTE, OCTOBER 20, 1944 (LIEUTENANT-GENERAL MAKINO SHIRO)
16th Division (Lieutenant-General Makino Shiro)
9th Infantry Regiment (less three companies on Samar)
20th Infantry Regiment
33rd Infantry Regiment (less one company on Samar)
22nd Artillery Regiment (less 3rd Battalion on Luzon)
16th Engineer Regiment (less one company)
2nd Company, 16th Transport Regiment
7th Independent Tank Company
16th Division Special Troops
Thirty-Fifth Army Depots units
Elements, 63rd Motor Transport Battalion
316th Independent Motor Transport Company
317th Independent Motor Transport Company
34th Air Sector Command
98th Airfield Battalion
114th Airfield Battalion
54th Airfield Company
2nd Airfield Construction Unit
11th Airfield Construction Unit
Naval Land Forces
Elements, 36th Naval Garrison Unit
311th Naval Construction Unit

OPPOSING PLANS

In the Southwest Pacific, Allied and Japanese leaders held diametrically opposed positions. For Washington, taking Leyte was a stepping stone to future operations against Formosa or Luzon, and a possible invasion of Japan. There were several potential landing sites in the Philippines. An American victory in Leyte would have a profound impact. Tokyo recognized that its empire was shrinking with the American advances through the Central and Southwest Pacific. Resources, lines of communications, and further imperial expansion were at stake for Japan if the Philippines fell. IJA and IJN leaders would then have to defend several areas against the Allies. This was especially difficult given the losses of territory and force hemorrhaged throughout the region in recent years as the seemingly unstoppable Allied juggernaut advanced.

MacArthur had to gather forces from the X and XXIV corps from throughout the Pacific. Forces from Nimitz's XXIV Corps trained in Hawaii for a possible invasion of Yap that was cancelled in order to take Leyte. Here, landing craft prepare at Seeadler Harbor, on Manus Island in the Admiralties, for the Leyte operation. (US Army)

US PLANS

MacArthur, as Supreme Commander SWPA, had begun planning for a return to the Philippines while in Australia. American and Filipino forces had

suffered one of the greatest defeats in the Pacific at the hands of the IJA when Corregidor fell on May 6, 1942. After MacArthur escaped from the Philippines, he had vowed to return. SWPA staff officers translated MacArthur's pledge into initial efforts for a future Philippine operation. These efforts began in earnest after the Allies took Buna in early 1943; its result was *Reno I*. The *Reno* series of plans examined a combined land, sea, and air campaign to liberate Mindanao and the rest of the Philippines, cut Japan's lifeline to Southeast Asian resources, and provide a springboard to invade Japan. As the Allies advanced through New Guinea and across the Southwest Pacific, GHQ SWPA developed these concepts into detailed operational plans codenamed *Musketeer*.

Musketeer planners speculated the best way to liberate the Philippines was through a systematic push from south to north. Each succeeding operation depended on the previous military actions to establish land-based air power and logistical support. The first target was Mindanao with an invasion scheduled for November 15, 1944. Next, Allied forces would advance to Leyte on December 20. Leyte's liberation would allow major airfield construction to support a follow-on assault against Luzon. Leyte also offered MacArthur the potential to act as a major supply base for the logistics needed to conduct sustained operations against Luzon. GHQ SWPA had estimated the first Americans would hit the Lingayen Bay shore on Luzon by mid-February 1945.

Despite the debate between MacArthur's push to liberate the Philippines and King advocating for Formosa, there was little opposition to taking a support base in the Philippines. Depending on Tokyo's reaction to the Leyte landings and available resources, the Allies could move against Japan along several fronts. The JCS decision to move against Leyte released forces identified for other targets to MacArthur. It did allow MacArthur to advance into the central Philippines, which would cut off Mindanao and provide support facilities in a fight over Luzon. A surprise Leyte invasion might allow MacArthur to land on relatively undefended beaches, assuming Halsey's reports were true. Unfortunately, ULTRA intercepts and Filipino guerilla reports indicated the Japanese had at least a division – the 16th Division – and support personnel totaling about 21,000 men. If the Americans believed that Leyte could offer a base to launch land-based air raids on Luzon, then the Japanese could do the same against American forces from bases on Luzon. Putting forces on Leyte also complicated logistical support and the ability to reinforce American forces from Morotai. The weakened IJN could still offer a spirited defense of the area that could affect American operations. Finally, MacArthur would have to rely on naval air power, until his engineers could establish working airfields. This meant entrusting the aerial supremacy, close air support, and interdiction missions to naval commanders under Halsey and Kinkaid.

Nimitz had temporarily transferred Halsey's Third Fleet with TF-38 of four fast carrier task groups to the Leyte operation. The Third Fleet would support the Leyte landings and the initial drive into the island's interior. It would also serve to intercept and attack any IJN force that threatened the invasion. However, issues with the Third Fleet's command and control created significant problems later in the campaign. The US Navy would also have to play a major role in stopping any IJA reinforcements reaching Leyte. Kenney and his Fifth Air Force did not have the sufficient range to use its land-based fighters based on Morotai, about 500 miles (800km) away. Kenney would have to wait until American forces took airfields on Leyte.

Although Washington had administered the Philippines for over four decades, military leaders still required detailed information to plan the Leyte invasion, Operation *King II*. Filipino guerillas, submarine-borne intelligence agents, ULTRA radio intercepts, aerial reconnaissance, and civilians willingly provided information about the island's defenses and possible landing locations. MacArthur's staff selected the northeastern coastal plains as the primary landing sites. Specifically, Lieutenant-General Walter Krueger planned on landing four divisions simultaneously along an 18-mile (30km) front from

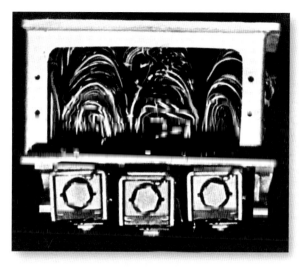

American cryptographic capabilities enabled Washington and its field commanders an unprecedented advantage in gaining information about Axis strategy and operations. In particular, commanders received ULTRA intelligence from a combination of sources. The "Purple" deciphering machine shown here, in a photograph taken between 1940 and 1941, allowed Washington to read Japanese diplomatic codes; the information gained was codenamed MAGIC. (National Archives)

Although American armor was superior to Japanese armor, tank crews remained vulnerable. The injured troops shown here are the crew of an M-4 that was supporting the advance of 7th Cavalry Regiment (1st Cavalry Division) on Tacloban Airfield. The crew had to evacuate their tank after hitting a Japanese landmine on A-Day. (US Coast Guard)

One of MacArthur's justifications for taking Leyte was that he believed the island would provide a logistical and air base needed for future Philippines operations. He hoped to use airfields around Leyte to conduct air operations on Luzon. His Fifth Air Force could then attack a number of Japanese-held airfields on Luzon to ensure the Americans could attain air superiority. (US Air Force)

Dulag to San Jose. Objectives around San Jose included taking the airfield near Tacloban and moving towards the San Juanico Strait that controlled passage between Leyte and Samar. Dulag also offered access to airfields inland to the invasion site and the ability to drive west across the island. A smaller force would land near the Panaon Strait at the southern tip of Leyte, which would provide access to the Camotes Sea and entry to Leyte's western coast. Landing on Leyte's eastern coast permitted MacArthur's forces to sail through the Philippine Sea into Leyte Gulf. If the Americans had attempted to land initially on the western coast, the IJN and Japanese air forces might contest the invasion force as it transited past Mindanao, Negros, and Cebu islands.

American planners made several crucial assumptions about Japanese intentions. Although GHQ SWPA intelligence officers knew of major IJA forces on the island, they believed the objective areas would be largely undefended since the Japanese did not have time to construct major fortifications, and because they would not consider that Leyte would be the point of initial attack against the Philippines. The predominant belief among American naval planners was that the IJN would not risk a major operation with her few carriers to protect Leyte. An important assumption was that SWPA officials did not consider the weather as a problem. However, known October weather patterns indicated 9 inches (23cm) of monsoonal rain for the month. Due to geography, the eastern landing approaches would face heavy rain; this would affect road construction, maneuvering, and airfield construction.

On September 21 MacArthur's staff released Operations Instructions 70 to implement the Leyte invasion slated for October 20. Krueger would translate MacArthur's objectives for Leyte into the following four phases. The first phase was to raid three islands at Leyte Gulf's entrance. The 6th Ranger Battalion would take Suluan Island, part of southern Homonhon Island, and the northern tip of Dinagat Island starting on October 18, two days before the main landings (A-Day), or A-2. The Rangers would silence any radio stations, delay any enemy detection, and capture available documents related to mines or beach obstructions. Controlling these areas would also allow the Americans to place navigational lights to guide amphibious forces into the Leyte Gulf. Additionally, the Navy would employ minesweepers and underwater demolition teams to remove any obstacles and gather intelligence on the beaches.

The second phase comprised deploying the major forces on Leyte on October 20. The X Corps, consisting of the 1st Cavalry and 24th Infantry divisions would land on the northern beaches. Meanwhile, Krueger wanted the XXIV Corps, transferred from Nimitz's POA, composed of the 7th and 96th Infantry divisions, deployed on the southern approaches. X Corps would take Tacloban Airfield, move against the San Juanico Strait, and then rush towards Carigara. XXIV Corps planned to move into the Leyte Valley, seize air bases near Burauen; and drive across from Dulag to Baybay. The 21st Infantry Regiment had the responsibility to seize the Panaon Strait. From A-Day to A+6, Krueger would maneuver and drive any defenders across the island.

MacArthur's forces would then initiate the third phase, A+7 to A+11, which would push through the Ormoc Valley and clear the island's west coast to Ormoc. American forces would also land on western Samar. The fourth and final phase, starting on A+12, would see MacArthur's forces turning against the rest of Samar.

JAPANESE PLANS

By mid-1944, the Japanese empire's earlier territorial gains had been eroded to a point where the IGHQ staff had to consider how to protect the Philippines and other vital areas from the oncoming Americans. Japanese senior officers viewed the archipelago's control as the first line of Japan's home islands defense against an American invasion. Tokyo viewed the Philippines as a vital element to ensure its access to oil, key natural resources, and food to keep Japan alive. Loss of these islands would isolate the Japanese Southern Army. On September 30, 1944 MacArthur's G-2 intelligence staff had estimated 224,000 IJA personnel stationed in the Philippines alone. Their loss would signal a significant blow to Tokyo and strike a dour chord to Japanese morale at home. Filipinos and other occupied peoples in Asia and the Pacific might become more emboldened to resist the Japanese with such a loss. However, fighting in the Philippines could force a major battle against the Americans. If Japan could win, it might result in a stalemate or time to build extensive defensive capabilities throughout the empire. This would not necessarily translate to a victory over America, but it would stifle MacArthur.

American forces had stormed the Mariana Islands by June 15 and then turned towards Saipan and Guam. With Saipan's fall on July 9, General Tojo Hideki's government resigned. The Allies had positioned themselves to cross Japan's "inner defense line" that threatened the empire. B-29s could bomb Tokyo from bases on the Marianas. The IGHQ started planning to halt further Allied advances. These efforts became the *Sho-Go* (*Victory*) plans that Japanese forces would execute once Tokyo approved their release.

This period Japanese artist's rendition of work in the IJA Southern Army area illustrates the conditions that Suzuki men had to work in. Hot, humid, and rainy weather made laboring in the jungles to build defenses quickly against the American invaders difficult. Although Japanese forces did build pillboxes and reinforced positions, they could only delay any American advance. (US Army)

The *Sho-Go* plan series consisted of four options based on geographic areas. *Sho-Go 1* concentrated on the Philippines. The second option included Formosa, the Ryukyu Islands, and southern Kyushu. The third option focused on Shikoku, Honshu, and Nampo Shoto. The last option centered on Hokkaido. The *Sho-Go* plans consisted of air, naval, and ground actions to stop any Allied movement into those respective areas. IJA and IJN forces would concentrate, strike, and prevent any Allied forces from establishing a significant presence within the inner defense line.

Part of the *Sho-Go* plans included a massive effort by Japanese aircraft to hit any Allied amphibious fleet. By July 1944, the IJAAF started training volunteers from its flight schools. The Tokko or T-Attack force aircraft carried at least one 800kg (1,763 pound) bomb. Japanese IJAAF bomber pilots received special training to attack at night and under all weather conditions to prepare sorties against an American or Allied fleet. (US Army)

IGHQ staff officers assumed that the first major Allied incursion into a specific area was destined to become the site of the decisive battle for the IJA and IJN. While the Allies hit the Marianas and Palau islands, and advanced through New Guinea and other areas, any major attack could trigger the start of a *Sho-Go* operation away from the Allied main attack. Japanese forces required well-coordinated and timed actions by the IJA and IJN. Given past and current issues regarding IJA–IJN coordination and cooperation, this assumption was problematic. Concentrating a sufficient force and the great distances involved represented a difficult challenge to Tokyo.

The objective of *Sho-Go 1* was to prevent a successful US return to the Philippines. Planners thought that MacArthur would move north from Mindanao, then to Leyte, through the San Bernardino Strait, and to the main prize Luzon. If the IJN could defeat the American naval forces during a landing attempt, then the Japanese might scuttle any amphibious assault. The combined imperial air, land and sea forces could then mount a counterattack to smash the Americans. Although the IGHQ created the *Sho-Go* plans, they could not control the IJA and IJN. Each service developed its specific version of the appropriate *Sho-Go* plans. The IGHQ staff did agree that coordination and cooperation had to overcome service parochialism to make the defensive efforts successful. Still, there was no overall commander to direct the Philippines defense.

Despite suffering massive losses throughout the Pacific, IJN leaders believed that a decisive battle, centered on Leyte Gulf, could crush MacArthur's invasion. They hoped to see the US Navy reduced to scenes like this. These survivors from the light carrier USS *Princeton* suffered at the hands of a Japanese Judy dive-bomber that sank the carrier on October 24. (US Navy)

The IJA's Southern Army was responsible for defensive efforts from Burma to New Guinea and through the Philippines. Protecting the Philippines was the Fourteenth Area Army's task with its Thirty-Fifth Army responsible for Leyte. From the fall of the Philippines in May 1942 until the summer of 1944, the IJA had put a minimum of effort into creating a defensive cordon around the Islands. Tokyo considered the Philippines as a logistical and supply base; it was also a staging area for operations throughout the region. IJA officers put more effort into the immediate front lines of New Guinea, the Marianas, and other areas under attack. Japanese plans did include constructing fortifications and airfields throughout the Philippines, but the Japanese troops assigned to the projects had to fight against guerillas and serve in garrison. By the spring of 1944, about 30,000 Filipino guerillas operated against the Japanese. As MacArthur advanced closer to the Philippines, guerilla actions multiplied and strengthened. There was little time and resources to build extensive defenses on Leyte. Besides, IJA officers believed the main effort to defend the Philippines was Luzon.

Japanese Army officers had learnt bitter lessons from fighting the Americans. If they attempted to repel any amphibious assault on the beaches, superior American naval fire support and carrier aviation would flatten the defenders. Instead, the IJA planned to create main lines of resistance away from the beaches to avoid American fire support. A defense-in-depth strategy took hold that would attempt to cause heavy attrition losses for any invaders. Using its reserves, the IJA would then counterattack and defeat the enemy.

IJN officers also applied hard-fought lessons to the Philippines. Instead of attacking American air power over the beaches and using surface forces to hit the landing forces on the beaches, the IJN changed strategies. The first objective was to destroy transports and carriers. Air forces played a pivotal role in these plans. IJAAF aircraft would strike the transports while IJNAF pilots would concentrate on aircraft carriers. After completing this task, the IJN could then focus on the landing forces. Without American aircraft carriers, the IJN could defeat the enemy invasion fleet. Tokyo would also use special night and all-weather air units to hit the Americans when they least expected an attack.

Conversely, IJN officers believed that the best way to defeat any Allied effort to retake the Philippines was an immediate, massive counterattack. The IJN would sortie its remaining fleet, in the region and home islands, and repel an attack on the Philippines. IJN leaders felt that if the Philippines were lost, then deprived of fuel and resources, the fleet would become useless anyway. IJN officers looked towards taking the first step by intercepting an American fleet and defeating it.

Unfortunately for the Japanese, they did not have the luxury of knowing where and when the Americans would land. The IJA and IJN had to react quickly to stem any invasion. However, in late August the Fourteenth Area Army staff projected that the Americans, based on air activity and weather conditions, would attack from the New Guinea or Saipan area between Leyte and Mindanao. It was only a matter of time before the Americans would return to the Philippines.

Filipino civilian labor provided a vital service to the American effort to liberate Leyte. Civilians supported road and airfield construction, but also operated in activities to support combat operations, like these supply porters who carried combat materiel across all types of terrain. This effort required a large pool of laborers to operate. (US Army)

THE CAMPAIGN

INITIAL MOVES

Before Washington ordered any further commitments beyond Leyte, MacArthur and Nimitz had to conduct some preliminary actions prior to any major SWPA amphibious operations occurring. Any advance north, including Leyte, required staging bases. MacArthur needed land-based air power for air superiority, close air support, interdiction, reconnaissance, transportation, and bombing missions. To allow some of Kenney's aircraft to reach the Philippines, the Allies planned on invading Morotai for its airfields. The island, south of Mindanao and north of Halmahera Island, was an IJN base. Similarly, Nimitz's ground echelon planned to occupy the Palaus, east of the Philippines to help future operations. The Allies invaded both on September 15.

Japanese Army officers speculated that Halmahera was MacArthur's next objective. The island's defenders had witnessed increased air raids, a potential signal for an invasion. In addition, Japanese air reconnaissance observed a large invasion force in Humboldt Bay, near Hollandia. This force consisted of about 110 ships bound for Morotai. Lieutenant-General Ishii Yoshio, commander of the 32nd Division, initially defended the island with two battalions, but later reduced the defenses to the smaller 2nd Provisional Raiding Unit. At 0600 on September 15, an American force composed of the 31st Infantry Division and 126th RCT (from the 32nd Infantry Division) readied to set foot on the southern tip of Morotai at Pitoe Bay. To forestall any Japanese reinforcements, Kenney's bombers hit targets in Halmahera, Mindanao, and the Netherlands East Indies. Additionally, carrier aircraft continually raided the Philippines, the Ryukyu Islands, and Celebes.

MacArthur's Morotai invasion was a success. By the 16th, American troops had secured the island's airfields. Ishii reinforced his Morotai defenders with three more raiding detachments to counterattack. However, the Japanese could not displace MacArthur. IJA soldiers did continue to resist until December. Kenney's aircraft flew sorties from Morotai bases starting on October 4. The Americans now had an airfield and a small naval anchorage capable of supporting an invasion of Leyte, Luzon, or Formosa. The 31st Infantry Division at Morotai could also act as a reserve for the Leyte operation.

Nimitz extended the range of his own forces by taking the Palaus, Marianas, and Ulithi. The capture of these islands advanced air, naval repair, and logistical support bases for future operations in the Philippines. Their occupation also served to protect MacArthur's right flank. The Palaus offered aircrews a closer location to operate against the southern Philippines. One island within the Palaus, Peleliu, was the site of heavy fighting. Nimitz's ground forces planned to take Peleliu to help MacArthur's original focus on taking Mindanao on November 15. Unfortunately, Nimitz would take about two months to subdue Peleliu, where both sides suffered major casualties.

Nimitz's forces also expanded into the Marianas by the summer of 1944. This move allowed B-29 Superfortress bombers to attack mainland Japan on a more consistent basis compared to ones flown from China. An American presence in the Marianas, like Tinian, offered a way to strike Tokyo directly, act as a base for future actions against Japanese home islands, and pull, more importantly, Japanese forces away from reinforcing the Philippines. Halsey's actions put to question part of the rationale for Formosa – bomber bases for use against Japan. By August, Marines had captured Saipan, Guam, and Tinian. The loss of Saipan, western New Guinea, and other Japanese holdings created a major political crisis for Tokyo. Tojo's government fell with the Americans penetrating Japan's inner defense zone. This Allied move towards Japan motivated Tokyo to take immediate actions to stop the American advance.

Americans also seized Ulithi, and it served as a valuable naval anchorage. This became a major logistical and repair facility for Halsey's Third Fleet, which allowed his fast carrier task forces and other naval forces to operate against the Philippines. The 81st Infantry Division's 323rd RCT took the coral atoll unopposed.

Along with gaining valuable support bases, Nimitz sent Halsey's powerful Third Fleet to decimate Japanese air forces throughout the Philippines. If these attacks were successful, then the chance of MacArthur's invasion fleet landing forces, conducting sustained operations, and sending reinforcements greatly increased. Similarly, Halsey's TF-38, Kinkaid's TF-77, and Kenney could strike Japanese positions, convoys, and Japanese air forces. Land-based medium and heavy bombers could hammer the Japanese. Naval and land-based air power also raked surface shipping targets that isolated the Philippines, reduced Japanese exports, and destroyed enemy transportation resources.

While MacArthur concentrated his effort towards the Philippines, Nimitz sought to expand Central Pacific operations. Nimitz ordered the taking of the Palau Islands. Here US Marines are on Peleliu, a particular bloody campaign. Washington did not cancel the operation despite the decision to go to Leyte. Nimitz believed that the operation, in part, might support the Leyte operation. (US Navy)

US naval air attacks

Halsey concentrated air attacks on targets throughout the Philippines. Admiral Marc Mitscher's TF-38 carriers conducted operations along the Philippine archipelago during the Morotai invasion and had greatly reduced Japanese air strength. From September 9 to 14, TF-38 aircrews pounded Mindanao and the Visayans, targeting Japanese aircraft on the ground and aloft. Mitscher's pilots destroyed about 500 aircraft out of a force of 884.

Later, the Third Fleet initiated attacks on September 20–21 against airdromes and shipping around Luzon, from where Japanese pilots operated out of 23 airfields. These strikes produced 205 more Japanese aircraft losses. Mitscher also hit the Visayans and Palawan on September 24. Continued bombardment took a toll on the Japanese. American anti-ship sorties in September reduced enemy transports by 50 percent. Navy pilots created much destruction. For example, on September 20, American pilots claimed 27 Japanese transports and 3 destroyers. Although Japanese officials tried to transfer aircraft replacements to the Philippines throughout the period, they soon fell prey to the TF-38 pilots. IJAAF and IJNAF air strength fell to about 350 aircraft.

Moving north, the Third Fleet smashed Formosa and the Ryukyu island chain, with carrier planes mauling the former island on October 9. American pilots then concentrated on Okinawa. On October 10, Mitscher's forces struck both airfields and aircraft. Pilots reported the destruction of 88 Japanese planes on the ground and Navy fighters downed another 23 Japanese aircraft in aerial combat. TF-38 carrier pilots also boasted of sinking 74 vessels. The next day, Mitscher hit Aparri on Luzon's northern tip.

One of the Third Fleet's major targets was aircraft and shipping around Formosa. The island also served as a potential source of resupply and reinforcements for the Philippines. Formosan bases housed major maintenance and support facilities for Japanese air power. If Halsey's forces could weaken Formosa significantly, then it might support the option to bypass Luzon and take the island. A large American naval presence also provided a very lucrative target that could entice the IJN into battle. Halsey might finally get a chance to dispatch the IJN's remaining surface fleet and its remaining carriers. However, recent American operations in the region gave the Japanese an indication of future plans; Japanese officers on Formosa could anticipate another Halsey visit. Nimitz planned to hammer Formosa again from October 12 to 15.

On October 12, Halsey struck Formosa. Tokyo reinforced the island with more aircraft in a futile attempt to counter another American strike, with the IJNAF sending 150 carrier aircraft to bolster defenses. These aircraft crews represented some of the few remaining trained, carrier-qualified pilots of the IJN's Third Fleet. IJN commanders could only count on 116 carrier-based planes for a major battle at sea. From October 12 to 15, TF-38 pilots pounded shipping, ground bases, and Japanese air power; Navy crews flew 1,180 sorties. B-29s also struck Formosa, dropping 1,166 tons of bombs in three raids. On October 19, the IGHQ admitted to having lost 312 aircraft. Allied estimates counted 396 Japanese destroyed planes. Overall, the Americans believed the Japanese aircraft losses from October 10 to 18 numbered 655 in the air and 465 on the ground – a major blow to Tokyo.

IJN Combined Fleet staff officers believed they could conduct operations against the US Navy as they had done in the past. Unfortunately, the IJN did not have the size or composition of warships as it had done in 1942 nor was the US Navy as weak. Japanese carriers, aircraft, aircrews, and warships were all in limited supply. To fight and win a battle against the American fleet was highly problematic by the fall of 1944. (US Army)

Japanese pilots did attempt to counterattack, with IJNAF and IJAAF aircraft focused on destroying TF-38. On October 13, Japanese pilots launched torpedo strikes against the cruiser USS *Canberra*, which caused heavy damage. The next day, the Japanese succeeded in torpedoing the USS *Houston*, another cruiser, which the Japanese hit again a few days later. During these attacks, Japanese aircrews made exaggerated claims against Halsey's forces. An IGHQ communiqué reported that the Japanese pilots had destroyed half the American fleet. This announcement included sinking eleven carriers, two battleships, three cruisers, and another cruiser or destroyer. The Japanese also believed that Halsey suffered additional damage to another eight carriers, two battleships, four cruisers, and several other ships. Japanese officers claimed 650 US Navy planes destroyed. Under these assumptions, Tokyo could now destroy any American invasion force against the Philippines or Formosa. Unfortunately for them, these losses were fictitious. The belief that the Third Fleet laid at the ocean's bottom would seriously affect Japanese strategy and planning, which would in turn undo the IJN and affect defense of Leyte.

MacArthur moves out

MacArthur's forces prepared to move from Hollandia and Manus to Leyte to support the invasion. The Australian First Army had begun replacing American units in the theater. The XXIV Corps diverted from Yap to Manus where it could join the X Corps Leyte amphibious force. At Manus, the XXIV Corps sailed, on October 11, under the III Amphibious Force with 267 ships. Naval transports also picked up the 21st RCT and 6th Ranger Battalion from Lae in New Guinea to support the landings. MacArthur's staff, Sixth Army headquarters, logistical formations, the 24th Infantry Division, and other units left Hollandia on October 13, in 471 ships under the VII Amphibious Force. Part of the VII Amphibious Force also picked up the 1st Cavalry Division at Manus. Both the III and VII Amphibious Forces rendezvoused on October 17. Minesweepers and other craft had preceded the amphibious flotillas to clear a path for them. There seemed to be no apparent obstacles for MacArthur to land on Leyte by October 20.

Kinkaid's Seventh Fleet covered the amphibious forces under TF-77. The latter consisted of 157 direct fire support warships: battleships, cruisers, destroyers, and escort carriers (CVEs). Eighteen CVEs served as immediate air power for MacArthur's land forces and as fleet protection. The fire support ships readied themselves to soften up suspected ground targets. One assumption made by TF-77 officers was that the IJN would not immediately oppose MacArthur's invasion, which affected the munitions carried on these ships. Kinkaid's ships carried 75 percent of its rounds as high-explosive shells and the remaining rounds as armor-piercing for anti-ship operations. Unfortunately, when the IJN did enter Leyte Gulf, Kinkaid's ships were at a severe disadvantage trying to fend off a surface attack by the Japanese without armor-piercing rounds.

Kinkaid's Northern Attack Force (VII Amphibious Force) and Southern Attack Force (III Amphibious Force) delivered the bulk of men and logistics to the Leyte beaches. Transports wait for the order to launch their landing craft on A-Day, October 20, 1944. (US Coast Guard)

Initial actions in the Leyte Gulf

A major pre-invasion task for MacArthur was to eliminate any major obstacles to TF-77 putting ashore men and materiel. These actions included landing on three islands in the eastern approaches to the Leyte Gulf to reduce the Japanese ability to detect the amphibious forces transiting to Leyte. Additionally, Navy ships swept mines, reduced landing-craft and transport barriers, and conducted beach reconnaissance.

Company D, 6th Ranger Battalion, readied to land on Suluan Island on October 17. In rough seas and tempestuous weather, Rangers stormed the beaches unopposed at 0805. The Rangers seized a lighthouse they believed to contain enemy mine charts and destroyed any radio equipment. Unfortunately, for MacArthur, a Japanese observer from the 32-man garrison radioed a message at 0719 to all IJN headquarters. The message identified a force of one battleship and six destroyers. About an hour later, Japanese radio stations received another message that stated, "Enemy elements have begun to land." The Americans found no Japanese in the lighthouse, but one man was killed by Japanese fire. Although the Rangers took Suluan, Japanese officers now knew the final American target was Leyte.

Admiral Toyoda Soemu, IJN Combined Fleet commander, reacted quickly to the Suluan report. He ordered the IJN, at 0809, to execute *Sho-Go 1*. The IJA also took action. The IJAAF initiated expanded aerial reconnaissance and launched attack aircraft to hit the invasion force. Terauchi pushed the IGHQ's IJA section to release *Sho-Go 1* for the ground forces.

Given the recent actions on Suluan and the American naval presence in the Leyte Gulf, the Army and Navy IGHQ sections surprisingly coordinated their response. The IGHQ IJA staff approved the Southern Army's request to implement *Sho-Go 1*. IGHQ officers determined that the coming decisive battle for Japan was the Philippines. One major difference was the battle's location. Terauchi, Yamashita, and other Southern Army officers believed it would be Luzon, not Leyte. With *Sho-Go 1* focused on Leyte, the Japanese

Preceding each major amphibious assault, the US Navy typically used battleships, cruisers, and destroyers to shell Japanese beach defenses in order to reduce enemy opposition. For Leyte, the TG 77.2 Bombardment and Fire Support Group lent its heavy firepower to smash suspected enemy artillery and troop positions during the days before and on A-Day. (US Navy)

would have to fight in the central Philippines, without extensive defensive works or major airfields. Yamashita would also use his limited shipping to send reinforcements to Leyte. If the Japanese lost Leyte, there might not be sufficient strength to defeat decisively any American offensive on Luzon. Deploying the few IJA units to Leyte would make a Luzon defense harder to accomplish. *Sho Go 1* could hand the control of the Philippines to the Americans.

Eventually, Terauchi agreed to the IGHQ position of making Leyte the primary location to fight the Americans. Believing that Halsey's fleet had been defeated off Formosa, Terauchi now thought the Americans could not sustain any major operations or contest reinforcement convoys, both poor assumptions that would later cause suffering for the IJA. Yamashita disagreed with Terauchi and the IGHQ about designating Leyte as the prime battle site. Even after MacArthur landed, disagreements continued in Manila. On October 22, Terauchi ordered Yamashita and the Fourth Air Army to make Leyte the main point of attack; his opinion was, "The opportunity to annihilate the enemy is at hand." Yamashita was convinced that the Americans had greater strength than anticipated, given the continued American carrier aviation's presence.

Contrary to earlier beliefs that Leyte was largely undefended by the IJA, some American units on invasion day faced opposition as they moved towards the island's interior. The 7th Infantry Division's 32nd Infantry Regiment moved towards Dulag on A-Day. Enemy forces built tank barriers, pillboxes, and other obstacles. Signs of heavy fighting, like the damage inflicted on this church, could be seen in Dulag. (US Coast Guard)

The 6th Ranger Battalion elements landed on Dinagat Island's west coast and moved north to Desolation Point at 0900. The force did not find any Japanese, and the Rangers erected a white navigational light for the amphibious force to transit to Leyte at night.

Meanwhile, Rangers in Company B planned to land on the southern coast of Homonhon Island. Bad weather and tides delayed the operation by 24 hours. On October 18, the Rangers scrambled ashore at 0915. Like Dinagat, the Americans encountered no resistance and secured it by 1038. The Rangers also installed a white navigational light visible 12 miles (19km) away.

Kinkaid's forces conducted minesweeping and direct-fire missions on the Leyte beaches. Naval personnel cleared mines throughout Leyte Gulf. The southern beaches received naval bombardments on October 18 at 1400 and the next day to allow transports to enter into Leyte Gulf at night on October 19 and 20. Japanese aerial reconnaissance flights had already seen transports and warships in Leyte Gulf. As the day progressed, Kinkaid's presence grew. The only question for Tokyo was when MacArthur's main force would come ashore.

Southern Army units stirred into action. Terauchi directed Suzuki's Thirty-Fifth Army to use the 16th Division to delay any American advance on Leyte. With reinforcements, the Japanese could then counterattack and defeat the Americans by October 24 or 25. The Fourth Air Army, along with IJNAF aircraft, could also throw itself against MacArthur and Kinkaid's forces. Since the nearest American land-based air forces were in Morotai and the Palaus, air opposition seemed minimal. In addition, with the apparent large American naval losses in Formosa, significant attacks by Halsey seemed unlikely. On October 19, Suzuki received notice that the 30th Division's 41st Infantry Regiment from Mindanao and infantry battalions in Cebu and the Visayas would reinforce Leyte. Victory seemed likely to some in Tokyo.

A-DAY: OCTOBER 20

The Americans initiated A-Day (October 20) with a pre-landing bombardment at 0600 off Dulag using three battleships. Similarly, in the northern landing area three battleships began shelling at 0700. After two hours of battleship fire, the cruisers and destroyers added their high-explosive rounds. The cruisers bombarded the beach areas from 0900 to 0945. Destroyers pounded suspected targets for 15 minutes. Both switched to inland targets at 0945.

American Coast Guard personnel captained landing craft that carried many troops, weapons, and supplies onto the invasion sites. At this beach, one can see Coast Guard-manned landing ship medium craft in the background that probably carried these troops' unit. At the far right, in the surf, is a 37mm anti-tank gun. (US Coast Guard)

Mortar and rocket-armed ships added their firepower. Then Kinkaid's CVE aircraft conducted bombing and strafing missions against suspected defensive positions and airfields. Navy pilots and gunfire smashed IJA artillery positions. The bombardment also severely disrupted radio-telegraphic communications.

The Japanese air forces responded with several attacks against the invasion fleet. Given the limited number of Philippine-based aircraft, 37 IJAAF and IJNAF planes tried to stem the invasion fleet. They accomplished little. Only the cruiser USS *Honolulu* suffered a torpedo hit.

H-Hour: Red and White beaches

By 0800, American transport ships had transferred thousands of soldiers onto landing craft. Krueger and Kinkaid prepared for H-Hour landings at 1000 across an 18-mile (29km) beach front. The X Corps' 1st Cavalry Division disembarked on White Beach, while the 24th Infantry Division secured Red Beach. Once the Americans accomplished A-Day objectives, X Corps planned to drive across the Tacloban Valley. The 1st Cavalry Division prepared to advance north from San Jose and seize Tacloban Airfield at

Landing craft first hit Leyte's beaches at 1000 on A-Day. Throughout the day, men and materiel flooded the beaches from Dulag to San Jose. Although there was no major opposition, in most areas, on the beaches, Japanese aircraft did try to attack the invasion fleet. Here soldiers and sailors watch American and Japanese aircraft fight it out over Leyte's skies. (US Coast Guard)

Cataisan Point. Concurrently, 24th Infantry Division infantrymen would aim for Hill 522 near Palo. This hill dominated Palo and a key road junction of highways 1 and 2 into the Leyte Valley and Tacloban.

Japanese opposition was light in the northern landing areas, although Japanese artillery and mortars did respond. The IJA's 33rd Infantry Regiment, less one battalion, defended along Palo to San Jose. The unit had arrived two days earlier. They lacked extensive defensive positions and failed to stop the landings and many American moves inland. American pre-invasion bombardment wrecked a few Japanese positions and forced a withdrawal from the invasion area. This allowed the Americans to take Hill 522. Similarly, the 1st Cavalry Division took control of Tacloban Airfield. Cavalrymen also captured a supply dump and forced Suzuki to abandon his headquarters and communications equipment in Tacloban. Despite the naval bombardment, Japanese defenders in heavily mountainous areas continued to resist the American advance west and northwest of Red and White beaches.

MacArthur fulfilled his promise to return to the Philippines. Coincidentally, he had arrived on Leyte 41 years earlier, to the day, to survey Tacloban as a junior officer. Accompanied by Philippine president Sergio Osmeña, MacArthur waded ashore at 1430 on Red Beach. While MacArthur visited the 24th Infantry Division, his party came under fire, but MacArthur

ABOVE LEFT
MacArthur's initial actions for Operation *King II*, the invasion of Leyte, had few glitches. Although the SWPA GHQ staff knew there was a significant Japanese presence on Leyte, despite Halsey's claim of few defenders on the island, casualties were low on the first day. Throughout the campaign, American troops would need support from M-4 Sherman tanks, like those in the background, to move against the IJA. (US Army)

ABOVE RIGHT
One of the immediate objectives for the 24th Infantry Division was to capture Palo. The city was a crossroad for highways 1 and 2. Highway 2 was a route to Carigara and a potential way to approach the Ormoc Valley. In this photograph, the Palo River separates Hill 522, in the background, and the city of Palo. American forces from the 24th Infantry Division's 19th Infantry Regiment faced intense fire from Japanese defenses as it approached Hill 522 on A-Day. (US Army)

In some of the landing locations the Americans found few Japanese defenders waiting for them on the beaches. Allied forces came ashore relatively unscathed by heavy losses, unlike earlier amphibious operations in the Pacific. Here 1st Cavalry Division troops take White Beach on A-Day. Beyond the beaches lay San Jose and the key Tacloban airfield on Cataisan Point. (US Army)

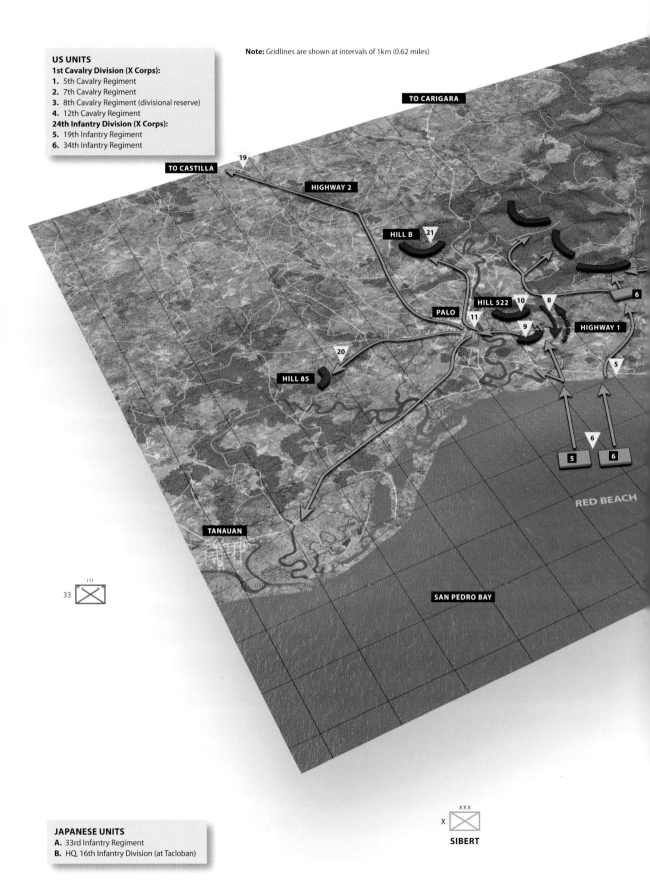

Note: Gridlines are shown at intervals of 1km (0.62 miles)

US UNITS
1st Cavalry Division (X Corps):
1. 5th Cavalry Regiment
2. 7th Cavalry Regiment
3. 8th Cavalry Regiment (divisional reserve)
4. 12th Cavalry Regiment
24th Infantry Division (X Corps):
5. 19th Infantry Regiment
6. 34th Infantry Regiment

TO CARIGARA

TO CASTILLA

HIGHWAY 2

HILL B

HILL 522

PALO

HIGHWAY 1

HILL 85

TANAUAN

RED BEACH

SAN PEDRO BAY

33

JAPANESE UNITS
A. 33rd Infantry Regiment
B. HQ, 16th Infantry Division (at Tacloban)

SIBERT

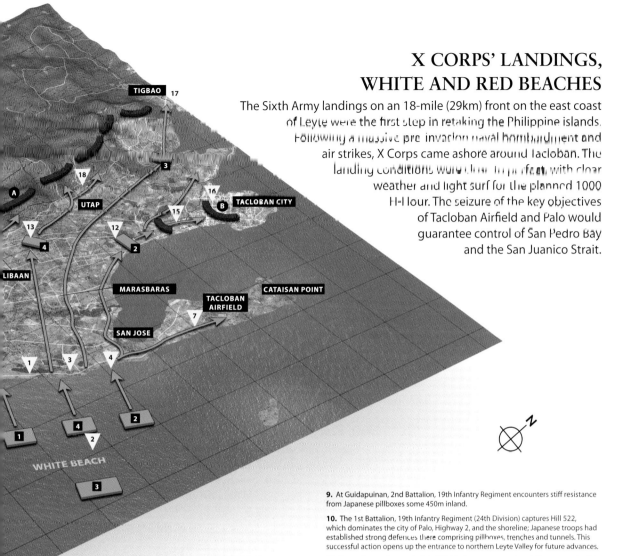

X CORPS' LANDINGS, WHITE AND RED BEACHES

The Sixth Army landings on an 18-mile (29km) front on the east coast of Leyte were the first step in retaking the Philippine islands. Following a massive pre-invasion naval bombardment and air strikes, X Corps came ashore around Tacloban. The landing conditions were close to perfect, with clear weather and light surf for the planned 1000 H-Hour. The seizure of the key objectives of Tacloban Airfield and Palo would guarantee control of San Pedro Bay and the San Juanico Strait.

EVENTS

October 20: A-Day

1. 0600–0945: All along the landing beaches, Kinkaid's Task Group (TG) 77.2 Bombardment and Fire Support Group and TG 77.3 Close Covering Group conduct direct fire support. Battleships, cruisers, and destroyers hit the coast to silence Japanese artillery and to shock any defending troops. At 0945, naval gunfire is lifted from the landing beaches and targeted further inland and to the flanks.

2. 0800–0945: LCIs are prepared for the landings. Rocket and mortar-barrage LCIs lead the way in the assault waves, and at 0945, 15 minutes before H Hour, they lay down heavy fire on the beaches.

3. 1000: The lead elements of Task Force 78 Northern Attack Force, comprising the 1st Cavalry Division of X Corps, land on White Beach. The 5th and 12th Cavalry regiments (1st Brigade, X Corps) land at the southern end of the beach.

4. 1000: The 7th Cavalry Regiment (2nd Brigade, X Corps) hits the northern end of White Beach near San Jose. The landings at White Beach are largely unopposed

5. 1000: The lead troops of 19th and 34th regiments from 24th Infantry Division land on Red Beach above Palo.

6. Japanese 75mm artillery and mortars strike the follow-on waves of landing craft off Red Beach, some 2–3km offshore. Four LSTs suffer damage and one catches fire.

7. The 7th Cavalry Regiment secures San Jose by 1230, then advances to secure Tacloban Airfield on Cataisan Point by 1600.

8. 1300: A platoon from the Japanese 33rd Infantry Regiment attempts to counterattack the 19th Infantry Regiment as it moves southwest towards Palo. The attack is repulsed.

9. At Guidapuinan, 2nd Battalion, 19th Infantry Regiment encounters stiff resistance from Japanese pillboxes some 450m inland.

10. The 1st Battalion, 19th Infantry Regiment (24th Division) captures Hill 522, which dominates the city of Palo, Highway 2, and the shoreline; Japanese troops had established strong defences there comprising pillboxes, trenches and tunnels. This successful action opens up the entrance to northern Leyte Valley for future advances.

11. After minor resistance in Palo, 19th Regiment troops seize a bridge across the Palo River. Despite this success, Japanese resistance west of the town slows movement for the 24th Infantry Division towards Carigara.

12. By the end of A-Day, 7th Cavalry Regiment has advanced 2.7km westward, and establishes its perimeter for the night.

13. Although the 5th and 12th Cavalry regiments have been slowed by waist-deep swamps as they push westward from White Beach, both regiments reach their objective lines by day's end.

October 21: A-Day+1

14. Elements of the 5th Cavalry Regiment approach Caibaan and the hills west of Marasbaras. American cavalrymen face intense rifle fire from Japanese defenders. The cavalrymen kill 13 Japanese. After facing more opposition and tough terrain, the 5th Cavalry receives orders to halt their advance into the hills.

15. Continuing their advance north, elements of the 7th Cavalry Regiment enter Tacloban, Leyte's capital. Japanese defenders have entrenched themselves in hills west of Tacloban and in the city.

October 22: A-Day+2

16. The 7th Cavalry Regiment secures the city of Tacloban. General MacArthur establishes the Philippines Civil Government in the city the following day.

17. The 8th Cavalry Regiment continues to probe northwest of Tacloban.

18. The 12th Cavalry Regiment pushes through Utap into the foothills to the west of Tacloban.

October 23–26

19. In 24th Division's move to secure the northern Leyte Valley, the 3rd Battalion, 19th Regiment begins its push towards Castilla

20. 1st Battalion, 19th Regiment secures Hill 85 on October 26.

21. 2nd Battalion, 19th Regiment secures Hill B west of Palo on October 26.

ABOVE LEFT
On A-Day the US X Corps came ashore in San Pedro Bay. The 7th Cavalry Regiment of the 1st Cavalry Division landed on White Beach near San Jose. The regiment faced relatively light opposition as it drove inland. Cavalrymen quickly moved north to seize Tacloban Airfield, a key objective to establish Kenney's land-based air power. (US Army)

ABOVE RIGHT
MacArthur, Philippine President Sergio Osmeña, Jr, and MacArthur's staff waded ashore on Leyte around 1430 on A-Day. MacArthur traveled in a landing craft, mechanized for a 90-minute trip from the cruiser *Nashville*. He asked a passing landing craft helmsman where the hardest fighting was occurring and then directed his coxswain to land there – Red Beach – with the 24th Infantry Division. (US Army)

continued to survey the beach. Soon after his landing, he made a radio broadcast to the people of the Philippines where he stated: "People of the Philippines, I have returned. By the grace of Almighty God, our forces stand again on Philippine soil." MacArthur later returned to the USS *Nashville*, which suffered a Japanese aerial attack. Despite his ability to call on hundreds of naval aircraft, this incident illustrated the need for air superiority and was a precursor of problems to come. Establishing airfields became a priority.

H-Hour: Orange, Blue, Violet, and Yellow beaches
The XXIV Corps deployed onto the southern beaches. The 96th Infantry Division planned to advance inland and take a series of hills north of Dulag after landing on Orange and Blue beaches. This included the Catmon and Liberanan hills where the IJA's 16th Division maintained some entrenched

Soldiers build a sandbag pier to facilitate beach unloading activities on A-Day. Logistical support and weather issues would later prove a great detriment to activities throughout the campaign. (US Coast Guard)

artillery positions. The 7th Infantry Division came ashore at Violet and Yellow beaches bordering Dulag. Those soldiers now pushed on to Dulag Airfield and marched south on Highway 1 to Abuyog. Taking Abuyog provided access to mountain roads leading to Baybay, on Leyte's west coast.

Japanese opposition was heavier in the XXIV Corps area since the IJA had planned on and prepared for the main invasion near Dulag. The IJA's 20th Infantry Regiment defended the city. The Japanese 9th Infantry Regiment and some artillery units protected the Catmon Hill area. As American forces approached the Dulag Airfield outskirts, they faced opposition. Artillery fire from Catmon Hill fell on the beaches

and the 9th Infantry Regiment engaged the Americans north of Dulag.

Another force landed at the northern tip of Panaon Island in southern Leyte. The 21st RCT took control of the Panaon Strait after setting foot on the island unopposed beginning at 1000. Control of the strait would contest any IJN movement of ships into Leyte Gulf.

Total American casualties for the landings at all three locations were light: 49 killed and 192 wounded.

A-DAY+1: ON TO LEYTE VALLEY

The next day, October 21, MacArthur's forces consolidated the beachheads. The next phase was to drive across the Leyte Valley. Unfortunately, not all went well with logistics. Although 107,450 tons of supplies had been landed on Leyte by the end of A-Day, it was a haphazard operation. Officers complained about the disorganized effort to deliver, store, and distribute supplies. This was a precursor of future resupply problems.

The next few days proved critical to the success of the Leyte operation. The 1st Cavalry Division units gathered at White Beach and then moved to Tacloban. The IJA's 33rd Infantry Regiment could do little to stop American progress. The cavalrymen focused on the San Juanico Strait to forestall any enemy reinforcements from Samar. However, the immediate need was to get Tacloban Airfield operational. Army engineers quickly started refurbishment activities. Unfortunately, the 1-mile (1.6km) long landing strip could only support a fighter group, about 75 airplanes, at this time. Kenney readied the 49th Fighter Group, comprising P-38s from Morotai, for Tacloban. Still, Japanese aircraft pressed their attacks and damaged the cruiser HMAS *Australia*.

MacArthur had some successes and setbacks. The 24th Infantry Division moved west of Palo. However, the 96th Infantry Division encountered swamps and met resistance in the hills north of Dulag. The division did succeed in occupying Dulag Airfield, but it required repairs. Another problem that arose was monsoons. Despite historical weather pattern reports, the SWPA planners believed the airfields could support immediate operations. Engineers had to install 1ft (30cm)-deep, hard-packed coral surfaces for drainage to make runways usable. Similarly, dirt roads, many one lane, deteriorated with the weather and heavy supply truck use. MacArthur's engineers had to choose between the airfield construction, road repair, and other projects.

Some of the toughest actions, for Krueger's soldiers, on A-Day were trying to gain inland objectives. For some units, this meant crossing difficult terrain. The 1st Cavalry Division had to move east across marshy ground that slowed their advance. These cavalrymen had to slog through a swamp to reach Highway 1. This obstacle forced many unit leaders to lighten their cavalrymen's individual combat loads. (US Army)

LEFT

Undoubtedly the toughest problem for an amphibious invasion is to get soldiers ashore safely on the first and subsequent waves of assault. Later problems occurred after the initial landings. On Leyte, thousands of tons of supplies and materiel hit the beach after units moved inland, leaving logisticians a tough job to sort, identify, and distribute the items. (US Army)

RIGHT

Americans from the 96th Infantry Division's 381st Infantry Regiment fought entrenched Japanese 16th Division defenders. Japanese artillery and infantry protected positions from the Labiranan Head to Catmon Hill. The area was finally cleared by October 30, but most of the defenders had evacuated the area to rejoin the 16th Division. (US Army)

The 7th Infantry Division's main strength moved west towards Burauen with its three airfields: San Pablo, Bayug, and Buri. The division would then strike north to Dagami. Opposition was still relatively light.

More problems surfaced. The IJN disagreed with Suzuki conducting a passive defense initially on Leyte. Unlike the IJN, the IJA had to move additional forces, with limited transports, to Leyte to build sufficient strength, to counterattack. This took time. Instead, Toyoda activated *Sho-Go 1* at the first sight of the enemy. He intended to destroy Kinkaid's invasion fleet and cripple the Third Fleet at the earliest opportunity.

THE BATTLE OF LEYTE GULF

If the IJN could destroy the American invasion fleet, then MacArthur's inability to receive aid by sea could leave him stranded on Leyte. It would also undermine MacArthur's amphibious capability to invade elsewhere in the Pacific. This would also eliminate the immediate threat to Luzon.

On October 20, Toyoda ordered the First Striking Force anchored off Brunei to the Leyte Gulf area to destroy Kinkaid's transports and escorting force. Under Vice Admiral Kurita Takeo, this surface attack force consisted of 7 battleships, 13 cruisers, and 19 destroyers. Kurita would surprise Kinkaid at dawn on October 25. Simultaneously, the Mobile Fleet under Vice Admiral Ozawa Jisaburo with the carrier *Zuikaku*, three light carriers, and two converted carriers would lure the American Third Fleet north. This would help Kurita deal with Kinkaid. Toyoda also used the Second Strike Force, under Vice Admiral Shima Kiyohide, to get underway from the Pescadores to Luzon. Shima's force was to assist convoys to Leyte, but this changed to supporting Kurita's move into Leyte Gulf. Toyoda also had the IJNAF's Fifth and Sixth Base Air Forces.

Kurita planned to hit the Americans both north and south. From the north, IJN warships would pass Palawan Island, through the San Bernardino Strait, and then enter Leyte Gulf. A detachment under Vice Admiral Nishimura Teiji, with two battleships and two cruisers, would separate from Kurita and push through the Surigao Strait transiting Leyte and Mindanao. Nishimura threatened Kinkaid from the south.

Kurita's moves into the Philippines ended with severe losses. On October 23 at 0634, off Palawan, two submarines sank the cruiser *Atago* and crippled the cruiser *Takao*. The submarines struck again at 0655, and holed the cruiser *Maya*. Reconnaissance aircraft spotted Kurita the next day. No Japanese aircraft backed Kurita's transit. American carrier aircraft proceeded to sink the battleship *Musashi*. American flyers heavily damaged another cruiser, the *Myoko*. Other ships sustained damage, but continued on their mission.

To Halsey, Kurita's future efforts seemed dead. Recognizing a chance to defeat Ozawa's Mobile Fleet, Halsey turned north against the IJN carriers. Kurita continued through the San Bernardino Strait and Leyte Gulf. However, Kurita had to delay for 12 hours and notified Nishimura not to expect his help with the attack. Shima's smaller Second Strike Force was steaming toward the Surigao Strait and could help Kurita.

Navigating into Leyte Gulf early on October 25, American ships ambushed him. Destroyers and PT boats unleashed their torpedoes. American battleships and cruisers, despite limited armor-piercing munitions, smashed Nishimura. Only two ships from Nishimura's nineteen vessels survived; they retreated. With Shima withdrawing, American ships and aircraft sank another destroyer and damaged a cruiser. The Battle of Surigao Strait ended as a decisive American victory.

Kurita sailed around Samar and slid into Leyte Gulf. Unexpectedly, the IJN fleet stumbled into Kinkaid's six CVEs, three destroyers, and a destroyer escort. Kinkaid ordered fighters and torpedo bombers into the air immediately. Kurita's ships struck the Americans and tried to smash the CVEs before they could launch their planes. The American destroyers fended off the Japanese surface fleet to buy time, and it worked. Navy pilots damaged three cruisers and Kurita thought a larger force opposed him; he pulled back unexpectedly. The Japanese again believed the Americans had suffered overwhelming casualties. Kinkaid lost only two destroyers, the destroyer escort, and a CVE.

LEFT
One of the most critical moments for MacArthur was the Battle of Leyte Gulf. IJN aircraft and ships attempted to defeat the American fleet. This would have isolated MacArthur's invading ground forces from support at their most vulnerable. Fortunately for the Americans, Japanese kamikazes did not destroy Kinkaid's CVEs, which provided air combat patrols over the fleet and island. Here a Japanese plane attempts to hit the flight deck of a CVE. (US Navy)

RIGHT
America's economic strength allowed MacArthur to provide massive logistical support to the Leyte operation. Although getting this support was problematic at times during the campaign, the US Navy was able to transport parts, food, ammunition, fuel, vehicles, and everything needed to fight on the island. Here LSTs line up to deliver supplies ashore on Cataisan Point. Tacloban Airfield can be seen on the left. (US Navy)

If Kurita had pressed his attack, he could have sliced through the American lines and raised havoc on Kinkaid's forces; instead he slunk north.

IJNAF and IJAAF aircraft did attack the American invasion fleet. Japanese air strength on October 23 numbered 50 aircraft in the First Air Fleet and 196 in the Second Air Fleet. The Fourth Air Force maintained 150 planes with 80 additional aircraft arriving the next day. Although MacArthur lacked Kenney's aircraft, Kinkaid still provided air support from his CVEs to the fleet and island. The 2nd Air Division mounted three attacks on October 24 against American ships in Leyte Gulf. They failed to sink any CVEs or destroy the invasion fleet.

Vice Admiral Onishi Takijiro, Fifth Base Air Force commander, took drastic action. With only a few aircraft and the need to eliminate the CVEs, Onishi ordered Japanese Zeros, strapping 250kg bombs, to dive into the carriers. At 1050 on October 25, five Zeros used suicide attacks against Kinkaid's CVEs. These kamikaze pilots succeeded in sinking the carrier *St. Lo* and damaging the *Kitkun Bay*. Another six kamikaze aircraft struck the Americans again. They hit Kinkaid's CVEs *Swanee* and *Santee*, but did not sink them. Kamikaze pilots demonstrated their determination to fight and were a portent of things to come.

Ozawa had little chance of defeating Halsey. He had only 116 aircraft on four carriers; 56 planes were operational. Facing Ozawa were Halsey's 17 carriers and hundreds of planes. If attacked by Halsey, Ozawa could offer limited resistance. About 200 nautical miles east of Luzon, Ozawa and Halsey clashed early at 0815 on October 25. Halsey's aircraft mauled Ozawa all day. The Mobile Fleet lost all of its carriers, three battleships, six heavy cruisers, three light cruisers, and nine destroyers. Halsey did lose the light carrier *Princeton* to a Japanese land-based bomber that struck the ship. Toyoda's gamble to defeat the American carriers and savage the invasion fleet failed.

SECURING THE LEYTE VALLEY

While the US Navy and IJN slugged it out at sea, MacArthur's forces advanced into the Leyte Valley. A key objective was the San Juanico Strait near Tacloban. The strait at its narrowest was less than a kilometer (1,100 yards) wide, and it separated Leyte and Samar. The SWPA GHQ staff had concerns about Japanese forces crossing the strait from Samar and threatening the northern beach landing areas. Additionally, IJA units could land at the top of the Leyte Valley and oppose the 1st Cavalry Division as it advanced up the San Juanico Strait. IJA reinforcements could also stymie the 24th Infantry Division as it moved towards Carigara, which controlled access to the upper Ormoc Valley. Krueger's forces had to move fast. Seizing Carigara quickly and later moving to Limon would allow MacArthur's units a means to move south and capture several mountain passes and ridges. Once Americans controlled those passes, they could move down Highway 2 to the island's west-coast major port Ormoc and block any enemy advances through the mountains.

Japanese resistance was relatively light around Tacloban. Elements of the 1st Cavalry Division's 7th Cavalry Regiment overcame about 200 Japanese defenders and liberated the city on October 22. The next day, MacArthur and Osmeña established their headquarters in Tacloban. Later, MacArthur announced the Philippine civil government's creation. Announcing a free Philippine government was easy; but hard fighting would continue. The 1st

Cavalry Division units pushed north to the San Juanico Strait. West of Tacloban, cavalrymen faced steep hills and difficult ground. Negotiating heavily forested areas also forced a slow advance. If the area was not secured, Japanese soldiers could outflank the Americans and retake Tacloban. As the 1st Cavalry Division marched north, it had to converge on Carigara. One way to do so was to cross a mountain range and advance to the city, but Krueger abandoned this option. Americans also had to secure both sides of the San Juanico Strait. This took time.

To quicken the advance up Leyte's northeastern shore and allow seizure of key areas, elements of the 7th and 8th Cavalry regiments sailed up the coast to secure two vital areas. On October 24, a 7th Cavalry squadron left Tacloban and took Babatngon. Japanese aircraft attacked a landing craft, infantry (LCI), but the Americans captured the town. Babatngon lay on the Janabatas Channel that connects the waters from Carigara through the San Juanico Strait to Tacloban. American soldiers made several other landings across Carigara Bay. Conducting amphibious operations, Krueger avoided difficult terrain, waterways, and Japanese forces. Meanwhile, the 8th Cavalry made another amphibious landing at La Paz, a ferry landing, on Samar. Other cavalrymen took Guintiguian opposite La Paz. Reinforcements, including tanks, pushed up the coast and then to Guintiguian. The 8th Cavalry reinforced La Paz and expanded south to the Leyte Gulf. The IJA 9th Infantry Regiment tried to attack the American beaches, but failed to dislodge them. The seizure of the San Juanico Strait succeeded. American casualties were relatively light with 40 dead, but Japanese killed numbered 739.

With the 1st Cavalry Division on its right flank, the 24th Infantry Division started out from Palo west across the Leyte Valley. The 24th Infantry Division could move via Highway 2, northwest through the Leyte Valley up to Carigara. With the rapid 1st Cavalry Division progressing along the Carigara Bay, Krueger started his drive on Ormoc. The 24th Infantry Division's task was to seize a road junction near Cavite. This junction split roads north and south. Taking the north fork, 1st Cavalry Division units that supported the 24th Infantry Division's flank could drive towards the coastline and link up with the 7th Cavalry moving west along Carigara Bay. With little apparent opposition, 1st Cavalry Division officers thought they could take Carigara. However, with an amphibious landing at Barugo, east of Carigara, and a land march, the 7th Cavalry entered the city only to find IJA units in position there; Army intelligence sources estimated up to 5,000 Japanese troops stationed in Carigara. X Corps officers decided to approach the city with the 1st Cavalry Division from the east and the 24th Infantry Division from the south. The 24th Infantry Division took the south fork, from Cavite and could then hit Jaro with a direct shot to Carigara. As the 24th Infantry Division

Sixth Army artillery units could provide devastating indirect fire support to American units during day or night. These 8in. M1 howitzers on Leyte could deliver heavy fire against enemy positions from up to 20 miles (32km) away. Despite poor accuracy and problems with barrel wear, this towed gun gave Krueger's men valuable support when land-based aircraft were scarce. (US Army)

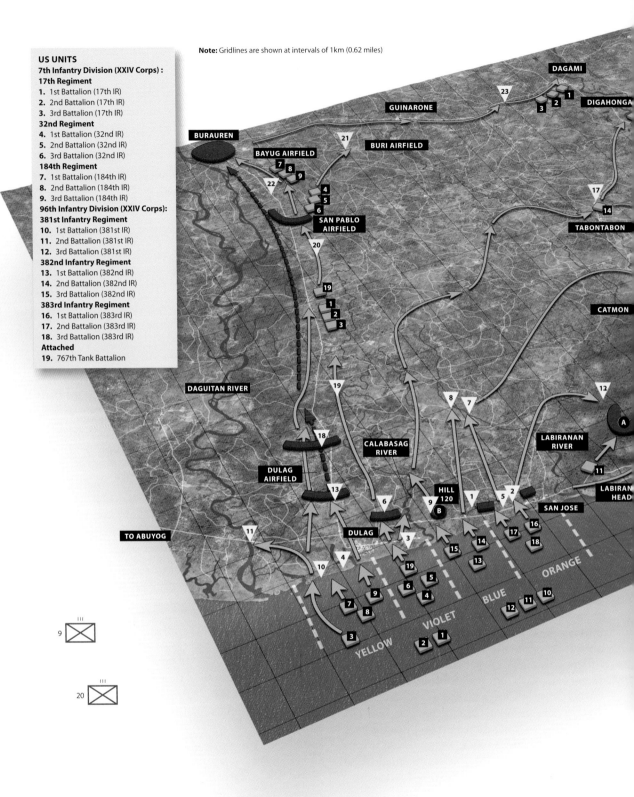

Note: Gridlines are shown at intervals of 1km (0.62 miles)

US UNITS
7th Infantry Division (XXIV Corps) :
17th Regiment
1. 1st Battalion (17th IR)
2. 2nd Battalion (17th IR)
3. 3rd Battalion (17th IR)
32nd Regiment
4. 1st Battalion (32nd IR)
5. 2nd Battalion (32nd IR)
6. 3rd Battalion (32nd IR)
184th Regiment
7. 1st Battalion (184th IR)
8. 2nd Battalion (184th IR)
9. 3rd Battalion (184th IR)
96th Infantry Division (XXIV Corps):
381st Infantry Regiment
10. 1st Battalion (381st IR)
11. 2nd Battalion (381st IR)
12. 3rd Battalion (381st IR)
382nd Infantry Regiment
13. 1st Battalion (382nd IR)
14. 2nd Battalion (382nd IR)
15. 3rd Battalion (382nd IR)
383rd Infantry Regiment
16. 1st Battalion (383rd IR)
17. 2nd Battalion (383rd IR)
18. 3rd Battalion (383rd IR)
Attached
19. 767th Tank Battalion

Japanese units
A. 9th Infantry Regiment (less one battalion) – at Catmon Hill
B. 20th Infantry Regiment (less one battalion) – in the Dulag area

XXIV

HODGE

XXIV CORPS' LANDINGS, SAN JOSE AND DULAG

Hodge's XXIV Corps had been ordered to secure the beaches in the San Jose–Dulag area. Once US troops had gained a foothold on the beaches, they were to move inland to secure Dulag Airfield and the three airfields lying east of Burauen. However, Thirty-Fifth Army commander Suzuki Sosaku believed that the main American landings would occur near Dulag and he had prepared defensive positions accordingly. In the dominating high ground of Labiranan Head and Catmon Hill, pillboxes, reverse slope artillery and mortar positions, and other entrenched defenses lay in wait for the 96th Division's troops.

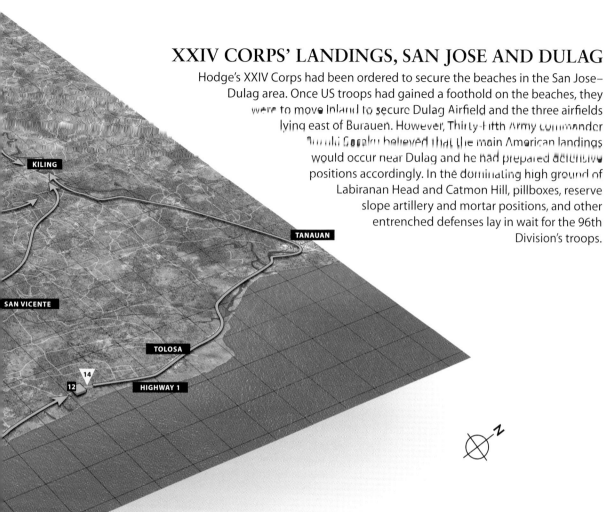

EVENTS

October 20: A-Day

1. 0950: Following a heavy bombardment, 96th Infantry Division (XXIV Corps) begins to come ashore. The 382nd Infantry is the first regiment to land, on beaches Blue 1 (3rd Battalion) and Blue 2 (2nd Battalion), under Japanese mortar and artillery fire.

2. 1000: The 383rd Infantry Regiment lands on Orange 1 (2nd Battalion) and 2 (1st Battalion) beaches. Japanese resistance is light.

3. 1000: South of the 96th Division, the 7th Infantry Division begins its landings, with the 767th Amtank Battalion in the lead. The 32nd Infantry Regiment lands on Violet 1 (3rd Battalion) and 2 (2nd Battalion) beaches north of Dulag.

4. 1000: On Yellow 1 (1st Battalion) and 2 (3rd Battalion) beaches, the 184th Infantry Regiment comes ashore largely unopposed; it moves rapidly inland.

5. 1045: The 3rd Battalion, 383rd Infantry Regiment (held in reserve) comes ashore.

6. The 2nd Battalion, 32nd Infantry Regiment overcomes Japanese small-arms fire and pushes west of Highway 1. However, the 3rd Battalion, 32nd Infantry Regiment is pinned down by heavy machine-gun and anti-tank fire from Japanese pillboxes.

7. 1100: The 383rd Infantry Regiment has pushed 1km inland from Orange beaches 1 and 2. However, progress is slowed here by swampy terrain.

8. Moving off Blue 2 beach, the 2nd Battalion, 302nd Infantry Regiment meets little opposition, and by the end of A-Day will have pushed 2.2km inland.

9. The 3rd Battalion, 382nd Infantry Regiment comes under heavy fire from Hill 120 as it attempts to move inland from Blue 1 beach. The 3rd Battalion (supported by the now-landed 1st Battalion) secures the hill by 1100.

10. 1300: The 2nd Battalion, 184th Infantry (kept in reserve) lands on Yellow 1 and secures the landings' left flank.

11. 1500: The 3rd Battalion, 17th Infantry Regiment lands on Yellow 1 and moves south on Highway 1, securing the crossing on the Daguitan River on the Abuyog road.

12. 1600: The 1st Battalion, 383rd Infantry Regiment crosses the Labiranan River and reaches the base of the Labiranan Head, where stiff resistance from the Japanese 9th Infantry Regiment forces it to halt for the night.

13. 1800: The 1st and 3rd Battalion, 184th Infantry Regiment reach the eastern edge of Dulag Airfield and halt for the day.

96th Division's advance, October 21–30

14. Having come ashore on October 23, the 381st Infantry Regiment advances inland. Its 3rd Battalion heads up the coast on Highway 1 towards Tanauan. It reaches the city on October 26, and then heads east, advancing to Kiling on the 28th.

15. 1st and 2nd Battalion, 381st Infantry Regiment secure the summit of Catmon Hill on October 29.

16. Simultaneously, the 383rd Regiment (less elements) attempts to envelop Catmon Hill from the west. It reaches San Vicente on October 30, and then heads north towards Kiling.

17. The 382nd Regiment (less elements) drives inland on a northwesterly course, reaching Tabontabon on October 26, and Digahongan on the 28th. The 382nd then turns northwest to link up with the 381st and 383rd regiments near Kiling.

7th Division's advance to the airfields, 21–30 October

18. The Japanese 16th Division withdraws from Dulag at 0300 on October 21. The US 184th Regiment takes control of Dulag Airfield later that day.

19. Moving in parallel to the north of the airfield, the 32nd Regiment covers the right flank of the 184th Infantry.

20. The 17th Regiment, supported by the 767th Tank Battalion, drives forward to secure San Pablo Airfield north of the Dulag–Burauen road on October 23.

21. The 32nd Regiment pushes on to secure Buri Airfield on October 27.

22. The 767th Amtank Battalion, together with the 184th Infantry Regiment, secures Bayug Airfield, and reaches the outskirts of Burauen on October 24.

23. The 17th Regiment pushes north from Burauen, through Guinarone, and reaches Dagami on October 29.

advanced north, more 1st Cavalry Division reinforcements would strike west from Barugo. The two routes to Carigara Bay for the 1st Cavalry Division and the 24th Infantry Division would entail traveling over mostly flat terrain, but would still cross several rivers that IJA forces could defend.

If Suzuki could obtain reinforcements, he could push Krueger out of the Leyte Valley. The initial American ground advance had steamrolled the Japanese defenders. Suzuki needed to regroup, prepare, and stage his counterattack. He decided to concentrate near Jaro and in the hills west of Jaro. Suzuki's move could halt the Americans from taking Carigara or he could cross over the mountain range to hit the enemy rear. The 16th Division's 33rd Infantry Regiment started to position northeast of Jaro. Soon, IJA units would land at Ormoc and advance to Jaro.

Yamashita and Suzuki considered several counterattack options. The Thirty-Fifth Army's planners counted on 1st, 26th, 30th, and 102nd division reinforcements. If the IJN could get these forces to Ormoc, then they would proceed north along Highway 2 to Carigara and hit the Americans. The IJA's 68th Independent Mixed Brigade (IMB) prepared to land at Carigara, but the landing was cancelled due to American control of the area. Suzuki hoped these actions could push Krueger towards the invasion beaches. To mute the XXIV Corps, Suzuki directed 30th Division reinforcements to attack Burauen. He wanted them to land at Albuera, south of Ormoc, and then use mountain trails to strike east. This plan assumed IJA reinforcements sailed unmolested. Still believing that the American naval forces had suffered a bloody nose, the Japanese organized reinforcement convoys. Another issue was the American capture of the San Juanico Strait and the 24th Infantry Division's northwest movement that could contest a Japanese counterattack. Still, Suzuki directed the 41st Infantry Regiment, 102nd Division units, and 57th IMB into the Jaro area.

American plans to capture Carigara went forward. Advancing towards Barugo, the 1st Cavalry Division units faced little opposition. The Jaro area was different. Although the 24th Infantry Division's 34th Infantry Regiment easily captured Jaro on October 29, the advance north proved otherwise. Japanese soldiers stalled the forward movement from Jaro the next day IJA troops sniped at the American infantry, which forced Krueger's men to call in armor and artillery support. The Japanese retreated, the Americans advanced. Suzuki's men employed artillery and mortar fire to harass the Americans. This encounter was a model of how to stall the Americans throughout Leyte. The Americans responded similarly. Relying on firepower and maneuver saved lives, but it slowed the American offensive towards Carigara. This tactic also put a drain on the logistical system.

Outside Jaro the 34th Infantry started marching north at 0800 on October 30. The Japanese contested the American move, and the 34th Infantry responded to enemy fire trying to stop the regiment. Japanese artillery and mortars hammered American movements within IJA observation. The Americans

Troop movements on Leyte were sometimes inhibited by dug-in Japanese defenders in entrenched positions. After landing on Red Beach and moving towards Palo, these 24th Infantry Division soldiers faced an IJA machine-gun team. The soldier on the right operates an M1918A2 Browning Automatic Rifle. Squads used these weapons as light machine guns for direct fire support. (US Army)

US and Japanese positions and movements from October 20 to November 2, 1944.

could go no further. Krueger responded with counter-artillery bombardments in hope of silencing the Japanese.

The next day, a 34th Infantry battalion executed a flanking movement northwest of Jaro. Soldiers cleared out and occupied a hill where Japanese defenders had stalled the advance the day before. The American operation succeeded, after three hours of combat. Cautiously probing northwest, the 34th Infantry faced another roadblock. This time, a pillbox, about 3 miles (5km) from Jaro, required an M-7 self-propelled 105mm howitzer to silence it.

The IJA's 41st Infantry Regiment responded. These IJA soldiers had disembarked at Ormoc on October 25 and had passed through Carigara on the 28th. Their original mission was to defend Carigara. Suzuki, at the time, still held thoughts that he could stage a counterattack. Any available forces, like the 41st Infantry Regiment, would screen and delay the Americans pushing towards Carigara. Japanese machine gunners from the regiment tried to block Krueger's men coming from Jaro. Night fell, and the 34th Infantry dug in. The 41st Infantry Regiment officers expected to confront a much larger American force than at first thought. They decided to move to the hills and regroup in Carigara.

Meanwhile, a new American plan to take Carigara arose. This plan included using the 24th Infantry Division's 19th Infantry Regiment in another flanking operation. The 19th Infantry had followed behind the 34th Infantry as a reserve unit to defend against a Japanese rear attack. This time, the 19th Infantry secured the road to Jaro while the 34th Infantry outflanked the Japanese. The 34th Infantry units started to move on October 31. However, patrols reported the Japanese had fled. The Carigara route seemed free of any Japanese and a link-up to the 1st Cavalry Division appeared likely. However, Filipino guerillas reported a Japanese build-up around Carigara with 2,000 to 5,000 soldiers in the town.

Suzuki realized Carigara was in danger of falling. He started to erect defenses across mountain passes where Highway 2 connected Carigara with Ormoc. If Krueger's 1st Cavalry Division moved faster, they could seize the passes and move south. Unfortunately, with the tough terrain, weather, and unknown Japanese opposition, American progress slowed. Suzuki also defended the mountain range separating the Leyte and Ormoc valleys as a natural barrier to any potential Sixth Army advance. Krueger could strike across the central mountains, but there were few passages through the steep ridges. The most likely avenue in the north for MacArthur was through Carigara, then Highway 2.

Suzuki's forces grew as Japanese reinforcements streamed into Ormoc. Still, the 1st Cavalry Division and 24th Infantry Division's advance expanded. As the Japanese 41st Regiment retreated, reinforcements from the 102nd Division, Tempi Battalion (57th IMB), 364th Independent Infantry Battalion (55th IMB), and 20th Independent Anti-Tank Battalion arrived and advanced towards Carigara. With possible amphibious landings behind Carigara and facing two American divisions, Suzuki's subordinates shelved the counterattack. The IJA in Carigara feared defeat. The Japanese pulled back to Capoocan on November 1. Due to communications problems, Suzuki was unaware of the situation and still believed he could counterattack.

The Americans did not know about the Japanese withdrawal from Carigara. American infantry and cavalrymen did take Carigara without enemy opposition on November 2. The northern Leyte Valley was now secure and Krueger had opened an approach to Highway 2. Major-General Tomochika Yoshiharu, chief of staff for the Thirty-Fifth Army, stated: "the loss of Carigara was a stunning blow to the Japanese defense plans." Carigara served as a major transportation, supply, and communications center in Leyte Valley. Japanese officers treated it as a tremendous loss.

The XXIV Corps also pushed west to take airfields and across the mountainous north–south range splitting the Leyte and Ormoc valleys. Krueger's troops still had to secure areas in the beaches. The 96th Infantry Division's attempts to take the area from the Labiranan to Catmon hills encountered resistance stiffened by 6,000 defenders. Pillboxes, determined IJA soldiers, weather, and supply problems slowed progress. Once troops liberated the Catmon Hill, they could start moving northwest to clear out the southern Leyte Valley. The 7th Infantry Division drove west to Burauen. A mountain trail leading from the southern Leyte Valley to Albuera on the west coast started near Burauen. The latter became an important objective to both sides. Sixth Army and Fifth Air Force officers viewed possession of Burauen's airfields as a way to improve aircraft deployment on Leyte. If the 7th Infantry Division, with 96th Infantry Division help, could take Burauen, they could capture Dagami. This action would conclude the Leyte Valley's capture. The 7th Infantry Division also made headway towards Abuyog, south of Dulag. They would eventually allow Krueger to move west, across a key road, to Baybay on the Camotes Sea and a potential route north to Ormoc.

For the 96th Infantry Division's 381st Infantry Regiment, clearing Catmon Hill took a concerted effort. Entrenched Japanese 9th Regiment soldiers grudgingly surrendered territory. Since A-Day, naval fire support and Sixth Army 105mm and 155mm howitzers plastered the hills. Coordinated American fire and maneuver allowed Krueger to make a slow advance. The massed fire from 45 tanks supported the 96th Infantry Division's capture of Catmon Hill on October 29. Mop-up operations continued until the 31st. The Japanese had fought hard. American troops discovered the area contained 53 pillboxes, 17 caves, and several defensive positions. Unknown to Krueger, the IJA 9th Infantry Regiment had pulled back towards Dagami and Burauen on October 27. The 16th Division officers realized that they needed to stop Krueger and headed towards the hills west of Dagami and Burauen. The Americans could now bypass remaining IJA defenders near the beaches and defeat them later at their leisure.

While the American soldiers fought at Catmon Hill, the 96th Infantry Division's 382nd and 383rd Infantry regiments moved northwest towards Dagami. Swamps, lack of supplies, enemy opposition, and pillboxes stymied the drive. The 382nd Infantry required six days to reach Tabontabon, a crossroads town. Two major roads led to Dagami and the other to Kiling. Both roads ended on a throughway that started on the coast at Tanauan and led to Dagami. The 383rd Infantry had served at Catmon Hill by blocking

Fifth Air Force aircrews perfected low-level attacks against surface targets. Typically, B-25 or A-20 aircraft struck targets in pairs. The crews could strafe or bomb a ship. For heavily armored ships, aircraft would release bombs at 300ft (90m) altitudes about 2,000ft (600m) from the target at speeds of 310 mph (500 km/h). The munitions would submerge and hit the ship's keel. Pilots would release bombs at 50ft (15m) altitude flying at 240–310 mph (380–500 km/h) for lightly armored vessels; the bomb would strike on the side of the target. (US Air Force)

ATTACK AGAINST AN ENTRENCHED JAPANESE POSITION (PP. 52–53)

The American push toward Carigara from Jaro seemed a relatively easy 7 miles (11km) by road. However, Japanese defenders slowed the road-bound American advance on October 31. One Japanese method of fighting the Americans was to build and fight from entrenched positions, like pillboxes. On Leyte, the lack of time and manpower precluded a massive defense-building program. Instead, the Japanese built log pillboxes with extensive trenches.

Elements of the IJA's 41st Infantry fought E Company, 3rd Battalion, 34th Infantry Regiment as the Americans advanced from Jaro. This IJA pillbox (1) and its connected trenches (2) dominated the local area where Japanese observers could direct artillery fire against American convoys headed north. The pillbox was on a knoll where the Americans attacked it with combined infantry (3) and the use of a self-propelled M-7 Priest (4) armed with a 105mm gun (5). One infantryman is attempting to unjam his clip by knocking it on his helmet (6). The Americans would silence the pillbox with the M-7, but the Japanese continued to hit the Americans with artillery fire and succeeded in disabling the M-7, which the 34th Infantry eventually had to destroy since they could not recover it. This scene represents the tough fighting that Krueger's men had to face against the determined IJA throughout Leyte.

Japanese maneuvers from the north. The 96th Infantry Division now aimed northwards to push out any Japanese and link up with the 7th Infantry Division in Dagami.

Japanese defenders tried to delay the advance, but could not stop the Americans pushing west. The Japanese had few forces since the 9th Infantry Regiment had pulled out from the east coast on October 29. This eased Krueger's situation for clearing the road from Tanauan to Dagami. The 96th Infantry Division could now offer its assistance to the 7th Infantry Division's offensive against Dagami. The main American combat effort fell to the 7th Infantry Division.

Facing the 7th and 96th Infantry divisions was the Japanese 16th Division. Lieutenant-General Makino Shiro, 16th Division commander, had initially deployed around Dulag anticipating MacArthur's main offensive thrust in this region. Instead, Japanese defenders had to contend with a sizable American western advance from Dulag to Tacloban. Sensing a larger American offensive than anticipated, Makino retreated west around Dagami and Burauen. Japanese units continued to oppose both American divisions. From October 20 onwards, Japanese units tried to slow the advance by fighting from trenches and pillboxes, using their limited armor, employing anti-tank weapons, and initiating night attacks. Given the intense heat and humidity, swamps and streams, dense foliage, limited supplies, lack of close air support, dependence upon direct and indirect fire support, and communications issues, American progress stalled.

American commanders faced other challenges. They needed to seize territory quickly before the Japanese started building extensive defensive works and received more reinforcements. The objective was to take three airfields near Burauen. After consolidating their positions near Dulag, the 7th Infantry Division, using combined tank and infantry maneuvers, pushed towards eastern Burauen early on October 23. The next day, American units had cleared the few Japanese defenders from spider holes and buildings throughout Burauen.

One of the airfields, Buri, involved a difficult fight. The Japanese 20th Infantry Regiment, 98th Airfield Battalion, and 54th Airfield Company had created a maze of trenches and pillboxes. Defenders fabricated 100-pound aircraft bomb booby-traps. Japanese small-arms and mortar fire stopped the 7th Infantry Division advance and the Americans had to dig in and fight against 1,000 Japanese. The Americans employed tanks, direct-fire support from mortars, and close combat to destroy enemy positions. However, night was falling and the Americans needed more time. The 7th Infantry Division waited to take Buri the next day. The 7th Infantry Division's 32nd Infantry Regiment kicked off the assault against Buri at 0700 on October 27. Instead of the expected Japanese opposition, the airfield appeared largely deserted. The Americans had evicted the last defenders. Japanese losses numbered 400.

While Americans fought at Buri, the 7th Infantry Division's 17th Infantry Regiment moved near Dagami. Pillboxes, American reliance on roads, bridge

MacArthur's men faced difficult fighting conditions especially during Leyte's monsoon season. Here an M-2 60mm mortar team prepares to fire against enemy positions near a Japanese pillbox. This weapon provided company-level fire support comprising high-explosive, white phosphorus, or illumination rounds. The M-2 had a range of more than a mile (1.6km) and a rate of fire of about 18 rounds a minute. (US Army)

Medium bombers, like these B-25s, could hit targets with their bombs, but their ability to use forward-mounted weapons was increased. B-25s with several nose-mounted .50-caliber machine guns could strafe ground targets at low altitudes. Some models also had a 75mm cannon to destroy aircraft, vehicles, buildings, ships, and surface targets. (US Air Force)

destruction, night attacks, improvised mines, enemy artillery and mortar fire, and determined opposition confronted the Americans. The 17th Infantry Regiment required four days to crawl 6 miles (10km). By October 28, American units seemed poised to enter Dagami. The 16th Division established its main defenses 1,000 yards (900m) south of the city. The Americans still faced IJA forces in hills to the west and encountered marshy rice paddies in the east. The 96th Division had also positioned itself near Dagami to reinforce the town. Japanese infantry created a web of machine-gun positions and pillboxes in the city and on terrain known as Bloody Ridge. Sixth Army officers estimated the enemy strength to be about 1,500 to 2,500 Japanese.

Starting early at 0730 on October 29, the 17th Infantry Regiment moved against Dagami. Still, the Americans pushed through the defenses. Extensive use of fire and maneuver tactics that included tanks, M-8 self-propelled 75mm howitzers, and flamethrowers cleared out pillboxes. At one point, Japanese defenders in a cemetery used crypts as foxholes. Flamethrowers and riflemen hammered the Japanese, but they required another day to clear Dagami. The Japanese finally withdrew. The 16th Division and other IJA units survived a mauling. About 3,500 soldiers remained west of Dagami. The 7th Infantry Division estimated it had killed 4,211 Japanese since A-Day.

With the 7th Infantry Division near Dagami, a battalion was sent south on Highway 1 towards Abuyog from the Dulag area. They encountered no significant problems to their advance. By November 2, elements of the battalion were close to reaching Baybay on Leyte's west coast.

As the Americans advanced inland after A-Day, they encountered stiffening resistance by Japanese forces. Fighting was especially tough near Dulag. The 7th and 96th Infantry divisions struggled initially with the enemy in the southern Leyte Valley. American commanders increasingly called upon greater use of indirect fire support to dislodge Japanese defenders throughout the campaign. (US Army)

Since October 20, the 21st Infantry Regiment had guarded the Panaon Strait. With no apparent Japanese land threat to the strait, a 7th Infantry Division battalion relieved the regiment for return to the 24th Infantry Division. Eventually, the 7th Infantry Division would move from the Leyte Valley to the island's west coast where they would prepare to drive north to Ormoc. With the capture of the southern Leyte Valley, the campaign to capture the island appeared to move forward.

KENNEY'S AIR POWER GROUNDED

Poor weather had taken its toll on Krueger's advance. Rainy, monsoon-like conditions confounded his engineers, and airfield construction at Tacloban and Dulag floundered. Landing conditions were still poor. Naval carrier aircraft, from damaged CVEs, headed to both airfields instead of ditching at sea. As the Navy pilots attempted to land on Leyte, 28 out of 72 planes ended up damaged. Without suitable land-based US air power, the Japanese could continue to launch air attacks. Limited American air power did contest the skies against the Japanese, but could still only provide a minimum of close air support to MacArthur's men.

While Japanese aircraft continued to reach targets throughout Leyte, Kinkaid and Halsey's forces had to depart the Leyte region to resupply. Kenney took over with his limited forces. MacArthur did persuade Halsey to maintain some of his fast carriers in the area when he withdrew most of his fleet on October 29. Kinkaid also left ten CVEs only by redistributing fleet supplies, but he also had to refit. Halsey ordered Task Group 38.2 to provide some carrier support and fire support since he wanted to secure Leyte Gulf.

IJNAF and IJAAF aircraft continued to pummel American positions. Kenney had 34 P-38s from the 49th Fighter Group based at Morotai deployed to Tacloban Airfield on October 27. Kenney's airfields still had minimal capacity. Three days later, only 20 P-38s remained, as Japanese air attacks destroyed or damaged several of the twin-tailed aircraft.

In response, Kenney deployed more P-38s from the 475th Fighter Group. He also assigned six P-61s from the 421st Night Fighter Squadron to counter night attacks. Kenney later replaced them with F6Fs from VMF (N)-541, which improved night patrol and interception missions to include strikes on Japanese night convoys. Kenney's pilots started to make a difference. Fifth Air Force officers, like CMH awardee Major Richard Bong, the highest-scoring American World War II ace with 40 victories, flew from Tacloban. However, the state of the facilities constrained the actions that Kenney could take. Thomas McGuire, the second highest-scoring ace, joined Bong. McGuire was awarded the CMH posthumously, having made 38 kills. While P-38s managed to intercept Japanese aircraft, they struggled to clear the skies of the IJAAF and IJNAF and they could not stop all the Japanese reinforcements arriving by sea at Ormoc.

LEFT
A critical weapon for Kenney to deploy quickly to Leyte was his fighters. One of his primary fighters was the Lockheed P-38 Lightning. The P-38 served on almost all fronts during the war. In the Pacific, it excelled with its range and firepower. P-38 Lightning fighters first flew from Tacloban on October 27. (US Air Force)

RIGHT
Compounding MacArthur's early problems on Leyte were the bombing attacks conducted by Japanese aircraft at night. Kenney sent Northrop P-61 Black Widows to intercept Japanese planes during the hours of darkness. Kenney also hoped to use these aircraft to intercept any enemy surface convoys. The P-61 had a three-man crew and was armed with 20mm cannons and .50-caliber machine guns. Kenney later replaced the aircraft with the more effective US Marine Corps Grumman Corsairs. (US Air Force)

Japanese air attacks continued to take their toll; bombing attacks disrupted airfield construction and caused aircraft losses since they were parked close together due to space limitations. Still, Army engineers with Filipino labor made inroads towards rendering the airfields fully operational. Pilots could now use an expanded 5,000ft (1,500m) runway at Tacloban on October 31. With a growing Fifth Air Force presence, the Americans improved their ability to intercept bombers; as a consequence, the Japanese relied more on night attacks. Another area requiring attention was Japanese kamikazes. Kenney's pilots and the naval aviators guarding Leyte Gulf could not stop all suicide planes. Japanese kamikaze aircraft struck the carrier *Intrepid* on October 29 and the carriers *Franklin* and *Belleau Wood* the next day. They streamed to Ulithi for repairs. Air superiority for MacArthur was still in doubt.

Ground commanders criticized Kenney's continued failure to provide close air support. During the early invasion period, naval carrier aviators had delivered direct support. For example, out of the 121 troop support missions from October 20 to 25, pilots flew 33 sorties in direct support of soldiers. With Kinkaid and Halsey's forces departed, Kenney's focus was on air superiority. He had eliminated most close air support missions until later in the campaign. As a result, the infantry had to rely on artillery.

With few naval forces remaining and little land-based air power, MacArthur could not stop Japanese reinforcements sailing to Ormoc. Suzuki continued to hope that these Japanese reinforcements might forestall the American conquest of Leyte. Fortunately, for MacArthur, the Japanese suffered intermittent communications problems between units in Leyte and Manila. Yamashita and Terauchi could not determine how the battle was taking shape on Leyte and where Suzuki needed reinforcements. Moreover, due to limited shipping capabilities, Yamashita could only dispatch additional forces piecemeal.

Nevertheless, *Sho-Go 1* directed all Japanese military resources to fight the decisive battle at Leyte. Reinforcements from Luzon sailed for Ormoc. On October 25, 2,550 IJA reinforcements arrived on Leyte from Mindanao, the first of several convoys that extended the fighting. Other reinforcements followed. However, Navy and Fifth Air Force fighters did strafe the convoys. Partial ULTRA radio intercepts and the situation on Leyte led to some confusion for Krueger. SWPA GHQ G-2 speculated that either the Japanese were sending in reinforcements to defend the island or the convoys were trying to load the remaining Japanese forces to evacuate the island. It was the former.

LEFT
Major Richard I. Bong, "Ace of Aces" (top American air ace in World War II, left), spent all of his combat tours in the Pacific. Bong scored twin kills over Buna, New Guinea with his initial combat victories on December 27, 1942 and went on to score a total of 40 victories during the war. During the Leyte campaign, Bong flew combat missions in P-38s from Tacloban Airfield. Another top ace flying alongside Bong for the Fifth Air Force was Major Thomas B. McGuire (right). McGuire was the second highest American air ace of World War II with 38 kills. Like Bong, McGuire was awarded the Congressional Medal of Honor. (US Air Force)

RIGHT
The US Navy provided combat air patrols, close air support, interdiction, and other missions vital to Kenney's establishment of his Fifth Air Force on Leyte. This Grumman F6F Hellcat fighter had proven its effectiveness by intercepting Japanese aircraft in the air and striking them on the ground throughout the Pacific. (US Navy)

Yamashita dispatched reinforcements to Leyte under the Japanese *TA* ("many") operation. HQ IJA fears of depleting Luzon's defense lessened due to false assumptions of the scale of recent American naval losses; the latter affected future planning despite horrendous IJN casualties. The IGHQ ordered the elite IJA 1st Division, based in Manchuria, to alter its original destination of Luzon to prepare for Leyte. American signals intelligence personnel did not detect the 1st Division's transit to the Philippines, while Halsey engaged in fighting the IJN, he missed intercepting or observing the convoy carrying the division to Manila. In a reversal for American cryptographic analysts, Japanese intelligence officers released false radio reports transmitted in open text that indicated the IJN fleet was heading towards Leyte. Halsey doubted the transmission's validity, but he sent the Third Fleet in search of the non-existent threat on November 1. The 1st Division arrived unscathed in Manila.

Japanese reinforcements would impede Krueger's ability to conquer Leyte swiftly. Given the initial success of landing and subsequent maneuver against the sole 16th Division defenders, Krueger could have seized Leyte faster without this opposition and would not have delayed MacArthur's Mindanao invasion. Japanese ships, conducting *TA* operations, delivered about 45,000 additional men and 10,000 tons of supplies, but not without cost. Some estimates have it that American naval and air forces sank approximately 80 percent of all Japanese shipping destined for Ormoc.

The 1st Division disembarked at Ormoc during the night of November 1 under convoy *TA-2*, with the IJN ferrying about 13,000 soldiers and their equipment. This was the largest Japanese reinforcement operation during the Leyte campaign. Later, the convoy ships transferred Suzuki's headquarters from Cebu to Leyte so he could directly command his forces. Kenney ordered 33 P-38s to hit the convoy. B-24s also participated and sank a transport ship after igniting its ammunition load. Landing the 1st Division greatly complicated Krueger's ability to defeat Suzuki; he would later muse that their presence significantly delayed the island's conquest. For Terauchi and Yamashita, every soldier, every piece of equipment, and every bag of rice sent to Leyte also depleted Luzon's defense. If Suzuki could not halt MacArthur, the loss of the Philippines looked likely. The only ray of hope for Tokyo was that the Americans would tire of bloody combat.

LEFT
As American air power and naval presence strengthened on Leyte, Japanese *TA* operations became harder to complete successfully. Although the Japanese tried to protect their convoys with escorts, these destroyers and other ships also became targets like the transports. American PT boats, land-based and naval aircraft, and other units started to pick at the Japanese convoy system. Here a destroyer sinks in November 1944. (US Navy)

RIGHT
Consolidated B-24s were a key part of MacArthur's ability to provide a long-range bombing capability. These bombers could hit deep inside Japanese-held territory, such as the attacks from New Guinea on a number of island targets hundreds of miles away. B-24 crews on Morotai hit targets on Palawan Island, Cebu, and enemy convoys in Ormoc Bay throughout the conflict on Leyte. (US Air Force)

US and Japanese positions and movements, November 3–6, 1944.

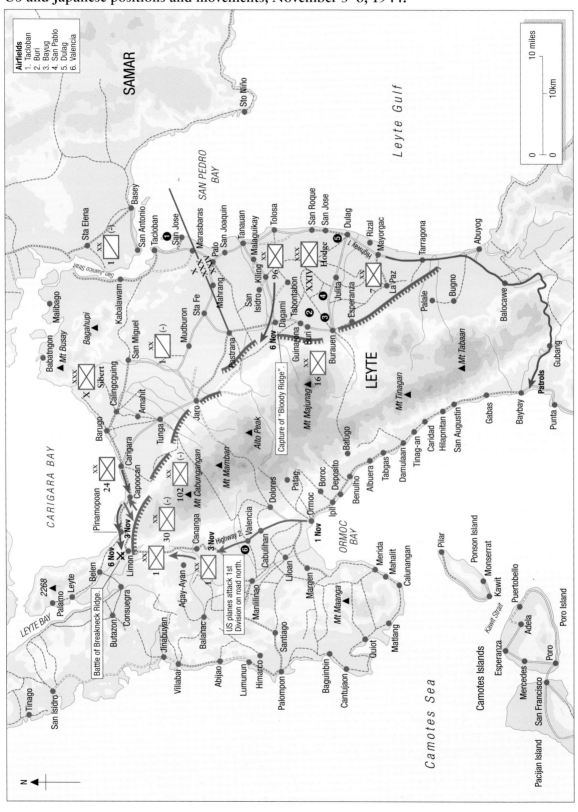

Airfields
1. Tacloban
2. Buri
3. Bayug
4. San Pablo
5. Dulag
6. Valencia

SAMAR

SAN PEDRO BAY

Leyte Gulf

San Juanico Strait

CARIGARA BAY

LEYTE

ORMOC BAY

Camotes Sea

Camotes Islands

LEYTE BAY

Capture of "Bloody Ridge".

Battle of Breakneck Ridge.

US planes attack 1st Division on road north.

Patrols

N

10 miles
10km

SECURING THE ORMOC VALLEY

With the Leyte Valley now secured, the next critical area to capture on the island was the Ormoc Valley. The Ormoc and Leyte valleys were separated by a central spine of mountainous terrain, and American forces would either have to traverse tough terrain or use limited roads to cross into the former valley. From Carigara Bay, the X Corps' 1st Cavalry Division and 24th Infantry Division could use Highway 2 to move south. Similarly, the XXIV Corps' 96th Infantry Division had an opportunity to use a mountain trail near Burauen to move to Leyte's west coast near Albuera. This option seemed difficult given the scant transport capacity and challenging terrain. Additionally, the 7th Infantry Division was starting to redeploy near Baybay, from where units could drive north on Highway 2 alongside the Camotes Sea to Ormoc. The Japanese 1st Division's presence allowed Suzuki to breathe new life into the island's defense. Krueger now faced Japanese reinforced units, well-defended positions, poor weather, spotty logistics, and limited access points to the Ormoc Valley.

The 24th Infantry Division would spearhead the offense from Carigara west on Highway 2 through steep peaks across the appropriately named Breakneck Ridge to Limon. Once at the base of the northern opening of the Ormoc Valley, Krueger would push through Limon and south to Ormoc. In early November Japanese units retreated west from the Carigara area. They started to position themselves in the hills around Limon and Capoocan. IJA units dug reverse slope positions allowing Japanese artillery and mortar crews to hit American units moving up the ridges and survive Krueger's artillery attacks.

Still, the IJA had hopes of regaining the initiative to push MacArthur out of Leyte. Lieutenant-General Kataoka Tadatsu, the 1st Division commander, resurrected plans to recapture Carigara. The 26th Division would then proceed to Jaro, while Kataoka and the other IJA forces would continue with an advance to Tacloban. Suzuki could call on additional 30th Division reinforcements to storm east from Albuera, on Leyte's west coast, through Burauen and eventually to Dulag. The 16th Division remnants, around Dagami, planned to assist this offensive. Kataoka also had 102nd Division units to support operations. The Thirty-Fifth Army could land the 68th IMB near Carigara, as a reserve. If the Japanese could assault quickly in sufficient numbers, then it might succeed. This assumed that these Japanese reinforcements could negotiate Highway 2 to Limon, a questionable proposition. Krueger was unsure of the Japanese dispositions and strength in the area.

Growing American air power started to reveal itself when Fifth Air Force planes attacked a 10-mile (16km) convoy carrying 1st Division units. The road convoy suffered the destruction of 30 trucks and 3 tanks on November 3. Despite the Fifth Air Force's Highway 2 troop convoy interception, Kenney did not attack with his full strength. Limited airfields still crippled Kenney. The Japanese had to stop American air power. Suzuki thought he could also limit American air strength by attacking Kenney's airfields. The IJA would later try to accomplish this.

The Japanese build-up continued. Krueger had to take a calculated risk. He now had to entrench on Carigara Bay, which allowed the IJA to expand their strength. X Corps began to probe the area south on Highway 2. The Sixth Army could move along multiple fronts to find any exploitable weaknesses in IJA defenses. This allowed Krueger to draw away Japanese strength in the Limon area and delay a possible counterattack. American naval officers were confident the Japanese could not land on beaches in the Carigara area. The IJN did not have sufficient resources to oppose major American landings. Despite these assurances, Krueger chose to slow his advance and prepare for a potential attack. Fortunately, he benefited from an improving logistical situation, and a limited, but growing Fifth Air Force presence. Another key capability Krueger possessed was his heavy artillery, to include 155mm artillery pieces, which could hit targets as far as Ormoc. Orders given to the 1st Cavalry Division and 24th Infantry Division were to secure, consolidate, and defend their positions against a Japanese attack. As soon as Krueger's men could adequately defend their positions in Carigara, he would then launch an attack towards Ormoc south on Highway 2 and coordinate a move up from Baybay with the 7th Infantry Division. Other Sixth Army forces could also cross the central mountain ranges separating the Leyte Valley from the Ormoc Valley.

The 24th Infantry Division's 34th Infantry Regiment had already pushed west across Highway 2 from Capoocan to Pinamopoan on November 3. Japanese forces could not evict the Americans, partly due to Krueger's ability to mass artillery fire. Japanese forces pulled back out of the coastal areas to the more defensible hills. Krueger could now exploit this opportunity and send forces through Breakneck Ridge. The 34th Infantry patrolled the Japanese positions around the ridge and encountered firm Japanese defenses. Reports indicated that the Japanese had created a trench system across not only Breakneck Ridge, but also from Corkscrew Ridge to the east.

The battle for the northern Ormoc Valley began with the Japanese 1st Division's 1st Reconnaissance Regiment maneuvering to stifle any American advance near Managasnas, below Breakneck Ridge. On November 4, the IJA regiment had collided head-on with an American force, but they could not dislodge the Americans. Heavy artillery bombardment forced the Japanese to retreat. Krueger relieved the 34th Infantry on November 5, but the enemy attacks continued while Krueger sought information about Japanese defenses. The IJA 57th Infantry Regiment, a unit of the 1st Division, took up the attacks on the 5th and 6th, but they failed. Krueger's forces redeployed to protect Carigara from a possible sea-based attack despite the Navy's estimate of an unlikely IJA amphibious landing on Carigara Bay. Krueger would first build up his defenses and then he could initiate operations to move towards Ormoc again. American units along Breakneck Ridge began to prepare for a tough fight.

Taking Breakneck Ridge

The Japanese 1st Division deployed above Breakneck Ridge and to its sides. The IJA hoped to deflect any flanking movement by the enemy. Krueger's task to push out the Japanese seemed Herculean. The only way to avoid a frontal assault up Breakneck Ridge was to use flanking actions from the east and west to envelop the Japanese on the ridge. This would take time and require fighting over tough terrain.

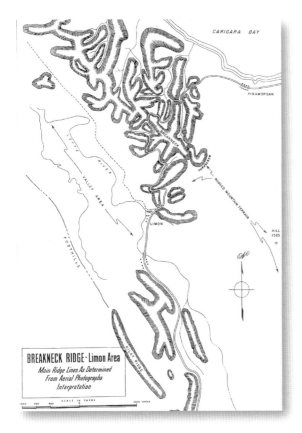

The area around Breakneck Ridge, northern Leyte. (US Army)

The US 21st Infantry Regiment started their move against the Breakneck Ridge area from OP Hill to Corkscrew Ridge. The Japanese 57th Regiment and the Americans launched attacks and counterattacks on November 5. The 21st Infantry Regiment had to retreat to the coast due to heavy IJA artillery and mortar fire. Despite massed fire from heavy artillery units, Krueger's men could not dislodge the Japanese 1st Division from Breakneck Ridge. The US 21st Infantry Regiment took days to make only a slow advance. Unfortunately for MacArthur, a typhoon hit Leyte on

November 8, which bogged down his attempt to eject Kataoka. Although the offensive stalled, signs of some success surfaced as American soldiers found abandoned field equipment that included a Japanese field order. This field order identified the Thirty-Fifth Army's future offensive to retake Leyte. Krueger now had to prepare for a possible Japanese counterstrike.

Japanese troops were forced, in many cases, to resist American movements in mountainous, jungle areas. IJA forces had to endure bad weather, dwindling supplies, and continued pounding by the Americans. This resulted in a downward spiral of combat capability for the Thirty-Fifth Army. Although the Japanese were a determined foe, they eventually succumbed to overwhelming Allied force. (US Army)

The heavy rain made movement difficult around Breakneck Ridge. Still, American infantry using flamethrowers and tanks struck during the storms. Krueger's infantry pried out Japanese defenders in spider holes, across entrenchments, behind destroyed bridges, against minefields, and other obstacles. The Japanese also conducted vicious counterattacks and sought any weaknesses in Krueger's positions. Krueger's attack slowed again.

With the direct approach stalled, Krueger used several flanking movements to take Limon and bypass Breakneck Ridge. The 1st Battalion, 34th Infantry Regiment, departed, by amphibious craft, from Capoocan on November 10 and moved west of Limon, behind a major range of hills towards Kilay Ridge, south of Limon, by November 13. Simultaneously, the 2nd Battalion, 19th Infantry Regiment, headed west, across the mountains to positions near Highway 2, south of Limon, arriving by November 15. The battered IJA 1st Division still controlled a series of ridges north of Limon that barred a direct advance. Simultaneously, American units started to pinch the Japanese out on the left and right flanks of Breakneck Ridge.

American efforts to reach Highway 2 and Limon came close to succeeding. However, Japanese reaction was swift and pushed back the Americans. The 1st Battalion, 21st Infantry came within half a mile (800m) of Limon before retreating to Pinamopoan. Direct fire from artillery and continuous fighting took a toll on the Japanese. Although Suzuki had stalled the American offensive, it could not hold out forever. Combined American tank and infantry efforts finally broke through on November 14 at Breakneck Ridge. Arguably, the fight for Breakneck Ridge was one of the bloodiest confrontations in the campaign for Krueger. The US 21st Infantry Regiment suffered 630 combat casualties while it inflicted 1,779 Japanese killed.

The Battle of Ormoc Bay

The IJN's inability to defeat the American fleet meant that MacArthur was not only able to continue fighting, but could build up his forces too. While the IJA was defending Breakneck Ridge, further Japanese reinforcements sailed south from Manila. Part of Suzuki's plan to retake Leyte was to deploy

US and Japanese positions and movements, November 7–30, 1944.

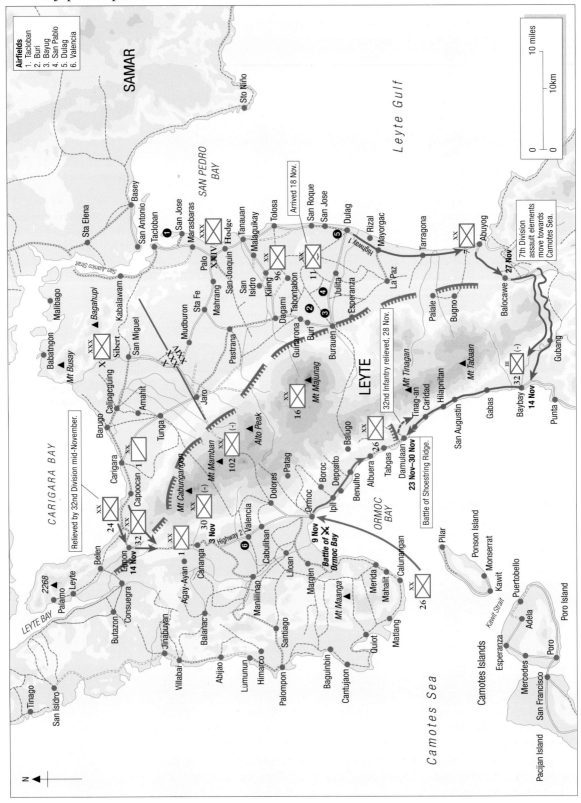

the 26th Division. The IJN organized two convoys to transport the division to Ormoc. The main convoy, *TA-4*, included 10,000 men from the 26th Division, about 1,000 1st Division soldiers, and 3,500 tons of munitions, it sailed from Luzon to Leyte on November 8. *TA-3* carried the 26th Division's heavy equipment and roughly 2,000 personnel, and it left a day after *TA-4*. The *TA-3* convoy also contained four long-range artillery pieces, a vital asset for Suzuki.

A combination of Fifth Air Force, carrier aviation under Halsey, and PT-boats attacked and sank several convoy ships. This American effort, known as the Battle of Ormoc Bay, concentrated on ending the Fourteenth Area Army's ability to transfer large-scale reinforcements to Ormoc. On the evening of November 9, as *TA-4* started to unload at Ormoc, P-38s from Tacloban and 30 B-25s, from the 38th Bombardment Group, struck. Flying low, the planes hit the main pier at Ormoc, which forced the Japanese transport crews to unload cargoes via landing craft. The Japanese transports became more vulnerable to aircraft since the discharge of personnel and supplies took time. Earlier, Kenney's veteran B-25 and A-20 crews had perfected skip-bombing techniques and applying medium bombers as gun platforms. B-25 crews flew at ship-mast level to improve strafing results, but this also put these medium bombers at greater risk from Japanese AA fire. The next day, more B-25s and P-47s hit the convoy. Fifth Air Force pilots sank two large transports and an escort ship. They also damaged several escorts. The Fifth Air Force did lose seven B-25s, to include one shot down by Halsey's pilots, and four P-38s. Japanese aircraft losses amounted to 25 planes. Kenney required more help with *TA-3*. On November 11, Halsey's TF-38 with 347 aircraft from 13 carriers attacked *TA-3*, resulting in three transports and five escorts sunk. The IJA units lost most of its equipment plus 3,200 soldiers.

As Sixth Army engineers improved the airfields on Leyte, the Fifth Air Force strengthened its presence on the island. Although the IJAAF and IJNAF continued to battle the Americans and attack airfields on Leyte, their air losses also started to take a toll. From October 28 to November 4, Kenney reported that the Americans downed 350 Japanese aircraft in combat and 120 on the ground in the Philippines. This was another stunning loss in aircraft and pilots. Although Japanese planes were still present on Luzon airstrips, the IJAAF and IJNAF had to prepare for a possible Luzon invasion, protect its airfields, and convoys to Ormoc. Tokyo faced tough choices.

The Americans expanded their presence into the Camotes Sea as the campaign unfolded. IJN losses started to tell, and convoys had to pass a gauntlet of American forces to arrive at Ormoc. Furthermore, ULTRA intercepts gave MacArthur an advantage: intelligence officers had identified *TA-3* and *TA-4* convoys departing Manila Bay around November 7, their strengths, and schedules. Cryptographic intercepts also tracked their progress. Japanese transports continued to arrive at Leyte until December 13 with five additional *TA* missions, but they were relatively small. As the campaign wore

This Japanese view of IJA and IJN forces making an amphibious landing at night could easily represent a *TA* convoy system near Ormoc. American naval forces, especially PT boats and destroyers, intercepted Japanese convoys at night. The Americans sank several Japanese transports and escorts, forcing the crews and passengers to get ashore by any means. (US Army)

on, the casualties among the Japanese ships grew and their destinations started to diverge from Ormoc to safer locations around Leyte.

Yamashita's doubts about sending more forces and supplies to Leyte were strengthened due to increasing shipping losses. Earlier, Yamashita had been concerned about claimed Japanese naval victories in Formosa and their losses in Leyte Gulf. If the IJN had weakened the American fleet, why were American carrier aviation assets able to conduct large-scale operations? Halsey's carrier aviation continued to pound Japanese targets throughout the Philippine islands. Leyte was certainly important to the Philippines, but Luzon was still the main prize. As American submarines, air, and naval power tightened their grip on Japan and the Philippines, moving further reinforcements to the Philippines became problematic.

With the Leyte situation deteriorating, Yamashita and Terauchi's staff met in Manila from November 9–10. Yamashita advocated allocating no further resources to this unwinnable scenario. However, the Southern Army commander continued to support the IGHQ position to stay the course. Terauchi directed Yamashita, on November 11, to help Suzuki with his planned counterattacks on Leyte by sending reinforcements. The IGHQ scheduled sending the 10th and 23rd divisions to support Suzuki by December.

Tokyo also had to replace huge losses in airframes and crews. Air units from the Celebes, the Japanese home islands, and other locations began to arrive in the Philippines. IJA and IJN staffs had agreed, on October 28, to release more air reinforcements to Luzon. The IJAAF alone provided 11 air regiments by December. The IJNAF stripped training units to restore destroyed forces from Halsey's continued pounding. On November 15, the Combined Fleet ceased carrier aircrew training. The IJN had lost a fleet carrier and three light carriers in the Battle of Leyte Gulf. Tokyo did not require as many carrier-qualified aircrews for the few operational aircraft carriers in service. Cutting the training capacity signified the dire conditions in which Tokyo found herself.

The 405th and 822nd Bombardment squadrons, from the 38th Bombardment Group, conducted a successful surface attack against the Japanese *TA-4* convoy in Ormoc Bay on November 10, 1944. During daylight, 30 B-25s sank and damaged several Japanese ships. The IJN destroyer *Akishimo* had her bow destroyed during an air attack. The 38th Bombardment Group lost 7 aircraft with 25 airmen killed, and received the Distinguished Unit Citation for its actions. (US Army)

Moving out of Breakneck Ridge

While Krueger pressed south, Suzuki's 1st Division tried to counterattack. The IJA's 57th Infantry Regiment attempted to reach the sea near Managasnas again, but failed on November 14. Similarly, the 49th Infantry Regiment conducted an assault toward Capoocan and Colasian. Japanese troops managed to reach both objectives. With the main forces from the 24th Infantry Division near Breakneck Ridge and two battalions behind Limon, the IJA's 1st Division was caught in the middle.

Although Suzuki's forces had suffered considerably, the Sixth Army had also seen its ranks thinned. Krueger originally assigned the 32nd Infantry Division to take Samar, but with few Japanese forces on that island, the division relieved the 24th Infantry Division on Leyte. It landed on November 18 near Managasnas. Fresh troops from the 32nd Infantry Division allowed the Sixth Army to maintain its forward momentum against the IJA's 57th Infantry Regiment. Krueger started to push the enemy off the heights above Managasnas.

Krueger then redeployed the 24th Infantry Division near Jaro, away from the major fighting. The Sixth Army also held the 11th Airborne Division, 77th Infantry Division, and 112th Cavalry Regiment in reserve. X Corps officers expected the 112th Cavalry Regiment to aid the 1st Cavalry Division. While the 96th Infantry Division guarded the southern Leyte Valley, 11th Airborne Division paratroopers took up positions at Burauen to blunt any Japanese advance from the mountains. Krueger also had plans for the 77th Infantry Division. He ordered it to make an amphibious landing southeast of Ormoc. This operation would allow MacArthur to capture Ormoc and threaten Japanese forces in the Ormoc Valley. If the 77th Infantry Division could then drive north up Highway 2, it could ensnare the Japanese 1st and 102nd Divisions.

American progress driving south from Breakneck Ridge was slow. The flanking movements bogged down again. Commanders now used frontal assaults to try to push through the Japanese. The American tactics were predictable. Heavy artillery fire followed a slight break in action, then an advance. This provided sufficient time for Japanese defenders to prepare for an assault. This tactic did avoid American casualties, but it also delayed any forward progress. Krueger later complained that his officers, both junior and senior, lacked an aggressive spirit to press forward. Still, the Americans had some success. The 32nd Infantry Division pressed towards Limon from the east, and they did succeed in crossing the Leyte River and approached Limon's outskirts. Krueger could now outflank the 1st Division. Suzuki had to use any available units to protect Limon. The 1st Division reinforced the 57th Infantry Regiment with its 49th Infantry Regiment, but it was not enough, and Limon fell on November 22. With Limon's capture Krueger now controlled Breakneck Ridge.

The 32nd Infantry Division troops engaged in close combat with the IJA. Using tanks, flamethrowers, and fire support, Krueger's men measured progress in yards. Japanese soldiers fought delaying actions and yielded ground slowly. They eventually fell back into prepared positions. The American soldier dug-in nightly and repeated the same process the next day. Inaccurate maps did not help. American officers had to call upon native Filipino citizens, aerial observers, captured documents, reconnaissance patrols, and Japanese prisoners to provide intelligence information.

Japanese defenders tried to reverse the situation. They struck enemy positions at night or late afternoon. After shelling American positions, Japanese units made assaults when the Americans were tired after their daytime attempted advances and were trying to get supplies. Fortunately for Krueger, Japanese logistics problems worsened. Food, ammunition, medical supplies, replacement parts, and weapons were sparse. Japanese artillery and mortar gunnery were neither as powerful nor as accurate as American 105mm and 155mm artillery fire. American superior firepower and execution of attacks started to take their toll on the Japanese and slowly forced them back towards Ormoc. However, Krueger eventually took weeks to break through to meet American forces moving up from Ormoc and close the vise on Japanese forces in the Ormoc Valley.

Part of the Fifth Air Force's success was its ability to adapt weapons to a particular situation. Existing aircraft did not perform as Kenney required, so he ordered field engineers to modify planes and crews to change their attack tactics. Here "parafrag" bombs slowly descend from low-flying USAAF planes, typically B-25 or A-20 medium bombers, against a Japanese airfield. (US Air Force)

SHOESTRING RIDGE, NOVEMBER 23–29

The American effort to capture Ormoc would be a disaster for the Japanese forces on Leyte. As US forces progressed up the west coast besides the Camotes Sea towards the vital port city, Japanese efforts to halt the advance intensified. At Shoestring Ridge, successive waves of Japanese assaults on the US 32nd Infantry Regiment positions would test the American troops to the limit. However, the Japanese shift of tactical focus to the assault on the Burauen airfields resulted in a move to the defensive, in order to prevent the Americans from reaching Albuera.

HILL 380

2

PALAN RIVE

9

TABGAS RIVER

TO ALBUERA

TABGAS

BALOGO

WANGOG

EVENTS

November 23

1. 1830: the Japanese 26th Division begins an attack on the US 32nd Infantry Regiment positions along Shoestring Ridge. Artillery and mortar fire pounds the American positions. The Americans respond with counterbattery fire from the 49th Field Artillery Battalion near Damulaan.

2. 2100: troops from the Japanese 13th Independent Infantry Regiment launch waves of attacks against Company E, 32nd Infantry Regiment, through the thick vegetation. Part of the ridge is taken as Company E is pushed back towards the Camotes Sea. Both sides then dig in for the night.

November 24

3. Company K arrives from Caridad to reinforce the 32nd Infantry Regiment frontline.

4. Battery C of the 57th 105mm Howitzer Battalion moves into position south of the Bacan River and suppresses Japanese troop movements on the ridge.

5. c. 1800: The Japanese 13th Independent Infantry Regiment launches a ferocious three-pronged attack on companies E, L, and K of the 32nd Infantry Regiment.

6 1900: Company L, 32nd Infantry, manages to repulse the Japanese attack with heavy casualties, but Company K, 32nd Infantry, is forced to withdraw to the foot of the ridge. Japanese probing attacks continue throughout the night.

November 25

7. Both sides send out patrols during the daylight hours. Company I reinforces the US frontlines between companies L and K.

8. 2200: the Japanese attempt a repeat attack on the eastern positions of the 32nd Infantry, but are beaten back.

November 26

9. Little fighting takes place during the day, but at 2100 the Japanese 13th Infantry Regiment executes repeated attacks, with the main push focused on the right of Company G, 32nd Infantry. After several hours of intense fighting, the Japanese are forced to withdraw. However, Japanese troops have gained ground to the left of Company G.

November 27

10. 0600: 1st Battalion, 184th Infantry, arrives in Damulaan to reinforce the frontline. It moves into position behind companies E and L, 32nd Infantry.

11. 1600: 1st Battalion, 184th Infantry has pushed forward and regained ground lost to the Japanese on the left of Company G, 32nd Infantry. Minor Japanese probing attacks continue throughout the night on the US frontline.

November 28

12. The 1st Battalion, 184th Infantry relieves Company F, 32nd Infantry, while the 2nd Battalion, 184th Infantry arrives to relieve companies G and E, 32nd Infantry, in preparation for its attack towards Hill 918. The 3rd Battalion, 184th Infantry is held back as the regimental reserve in San Agustin to the south.

13. The relieved 32nd Infantry Regiment falls back to Tinagan.

14. 1945: elements of the Japanese 26th Division attack the right flank of the 184th Infantry Regiment, from the southeast and northeast, pushing it back a short distance.

November 29

15. 0900: Company A, 1st Battalion and Company F, 2nd Battalion, 184th Infantry Regiment, attack to retake the ground lost by Company G, 32nd Infantry Regiment. Fighting continues for the rest of the day in what becomes known as the "Bloody Bamboo Thicket." By the following morning, the US troops have overrun the Japanese positions and reestablished control over Shoestring Ridge.

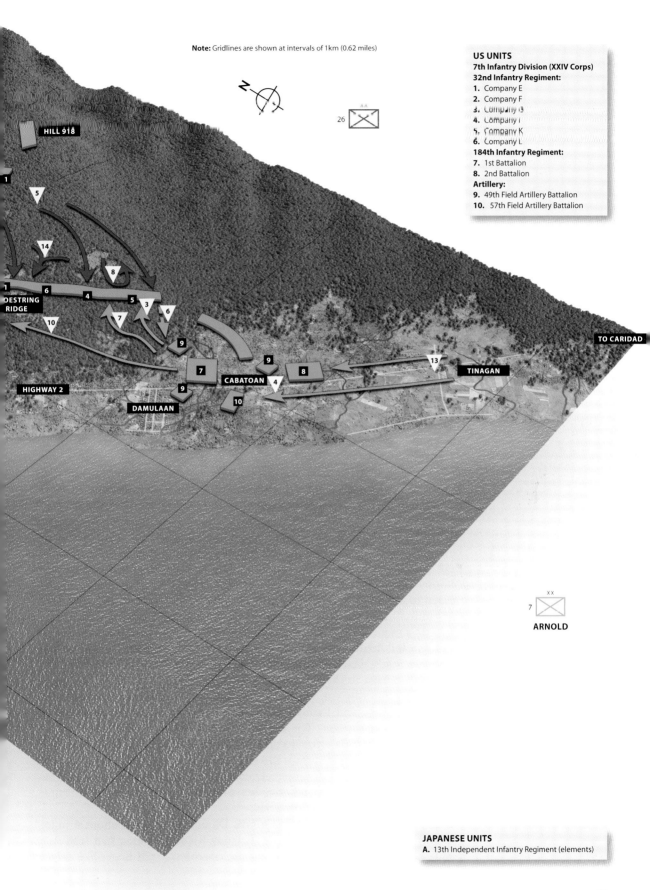

Note: Gridlines are shown at intervals of 1km (0.62 miles)

HILL 918

1

5

14

8

6

4

5

3

6

OESTRING
RIDGE

10

7

9

9

CABATOAN

4

8

7

13

TINAGAN

TO CARIDAD

HIGHWAY 2

9

10

DAMULAAN

26

7

ARNOLD

US UNITS
7th Infantry Division (XXIV Corps)
32nd Infantry Regiment:
1. Company E
2. Company F
3. Company G
4. Company I
5. Company K
6. Company L
184th Infantry Regiment:
7. 1st Battalion
8. 2nd Battalion
Artillery:
9. 49th Field Artillery Battalion
10. 57th Field Artillery Battalion

JAPANESE UNITS
A. 13th Independent Infantry Regiment (elements)

Crawling up the west coast: Shoestring Ridge

Krueger found few Japanese Thirty-Fifth Army units on Leyte's west coast when the 7th Infantry Division started to move westward to Baybay. The Japanese 1st and 102nd divisions were engaged north of Ormoc trying to stop the American push south, leaving the west coast relatively undefended. With the 7th Infantry Division now in Baybay and beginning to drive north, Suzuki changed plans. He realized that retaking Carigara was infeasible. However, Krueger's 7th Infantry Division appeared poised to conquer Ormoc. Any Japanese 26th Division replacements, which had landed in Ormoc and were destined originally for Carigara, could now be used to check an advance by the US 7th Infantry Division from the south. On November 13, Suzuki received a Fourteenth Area Army directive to send the 26th Division southeast of Ormoc to block an American advance north from Baybay. Their move could also forestall any American effort to interfere with a Japanese counterattack across the mountains. Suzuki thought of another option, namely hitting Burauen and advancing on Dulag. Future *TA* convoys could divert to Albuera to help operations against Burauen.

Moving from Baybay north towards Ormoc would not be an easy ride for Krueger with the Japanese 26th Division obstructing the 7th Infantry Division. American units had to cross numerous streams and towns where Japanese forces could barricade themselves. A more serious problem was terrain. The coastal road leading to Ormoc passed through a flat, narrow plain accented with steep coastal ridges. Japanese units could easily obstruct any American advance by holding important ridges dominating the coast road and launching counterattacks or bringing down mortar fire.

Suzuki first detached the 13th Independent Infantry Regiment from the 26th Division south to make contact with the 7th Infantry Division. Smaller IJA units tried to reach the 7th Infantry Division piecemeal, but all were defeated. With the IJA's 26th Division in the vicinity of Albuera, Krueger could not send the entire 7th Infantry Division from Burauen across the island. He could only do so on November 22 when the 11th Airborne Division was in place. Once the 7th Infantry Division had redeployed west, they moved north. Krueger's lead 7th Infantry Division unit was the 32nd Infantry Regiment. American soldiers had started to push north up the coastal road on November 14. Patrols encountered some Japanese defenders, but outnumbered IJA units could not halt the American advance.

Leyte's roads slowed Krueger. The "highways" were hard to travel due to their limited load capacity, and engineers had problems maintaining secondary roads, which were smaller than highways 1 and 2. Getting supplies and replacements to the 7th Infantry Division was a difficult proposition. Logistical support by sea was not an option: Naval advisers still considered IJN surface ships and kamikazes as major threats to American shipping plying the Camotes Sea. There was also a transport vessel shortage as MacArthur readied his forces to take Mindoro in December. This translated into no immediate naval surface fire support against the IJA's 26th Division. Until the Americans could completely control the air and sweep the Camotes Sea of Japanese destroyers and other warships, Kinkaid was hesitant to enter the western Leyte coastal approaches.

American forces had deployed above Damulaan, a town about 4 miles (6.5km) south of Albuera, near the Palanas River. The area had lush rice paddies, thick bamboo growths along the riverbanks, and finger-like ridges reaching out to the sea. Krueger ordered the 7th Infantry Division to halt and wait until notified to advance on Ormoc. The 32nd Infantry Regiment prepared positions south of the Palanas River and along a spine known at Shoestring Ridge. Two Japanese battalions defended the area, but only one maintained a defensive posture while the other was in reserve. Filipino guerillas supplemented the American forces. Krueger could also throw in another battalion from the 184th Infantry Regiment in an emergency. Soldiers from the 2nd Battalion, 32nd Infantry Regiment held positions about 1.5 miles (2.4km) in length from Shoestring Ridge to the sea. The hilly terrain and grassy areas could mask any Japanese movement. In addition, American officers had witnessed IJN ships and barges in the waters off Damulaan. Two 105mm howitzer batteries from the Army's 49th Field Artillery Battalion and one battery of 155mm howitzers from the 11th Marine Gun Battalion positioned themselves in the area. These artillery units would later provide vital fire support.

While the 7th Infantry Division guarded Damulaan, the IJA's 13th Independent Infantry Regiment massed forces across the ridgeline north of the Palanas River. Filipino civilians and guerillas noticed a large Japanese force build-up in the area and reported these activities. Despite the battalion strength, the Americans and Filipinos could not create a continuous defensive line along Shoestring Ridge, in spite of an anticipated major Japanese offensive.

Japanese artillery and mortar fire initiated the fighting at Shoestring Ridge. On November 23, at about 1830, the Japanese pushed the Americans off the ridge and tried to take Damulaan. If the Japanese could sweep the defenders off the ridge, they could envelop the 2nd Battalion and perhaps capture the heavy artillery pieces. By 2100, Japanese soldiers were streaming across the Palanas River and up the ridge. Lieutenant-Colonel John Finn, 32nd Infantry Regiment commander, withdrew from the ridge to positions near Damulaan. Finn's men hugged the coast and survived a night of attacks; they then counterattacked, and managed to regain some territory. Two reserve companies from the 2nd Battalion moved forward to reinforce the three companies holding off the Japanese.

After another massive night artillery and mortar bombardment, the Japanese soldiers hit the 32nd Infantry Regiment on November 24. This time, Japanese shells rained down on the artillery units near Damulaan. The Japanese failed to defeat the Americans. Over the next few days, the battle raged between the American defenders using heavy fire support and the Japanese trying to overrun their positions. Fighting was intense with over 400 Japanese killed during a November 26 night attack; but the Americans hung on.

Krueger needed more men to overcome Suzuki's opposition. He would now try to advance line abreast with two regiments and tanks. His men had to remove enemy soldiers dug in on the same ridges that they had defended. After several days of sharp fighting, the 184th Infantry Regiment relieved the 32nd Infantry on November 28. Despite the Japanese being entrenched in reverse slope positions, the Americans made a grinding advance north. The Americans finally recaptured Shoestring Ridge on November 30. Fighting at Shoestring

Army transportation officers used all manner of resources to get supplies to the front on Leyte. Mud, poor weather, and insufficient road-carrying capacity forced MacArthur's staff to use Filipino civilian labor to transport everything from C-rations to ammunition across rivers, hills, and jungles. This effort was effective, but slowed down operations. (US Army)

AMPHIBIOUS ATTACK OFFSHORE FROM BALUGO (PP. 72–73)

A determined Japanese defense, by elements of the IJA's 26th Division, delayed the American 7th Infantry Division from moving north to Ormoc. Krueger ordered Lieutenant-Colonel O'Neill Kane, 776th Amphibian Tank Battalion commander, to attack Japanese artillery positions that were harassing American positions near Shoestring Ridge. At 0635 on December 3, 18 LVT (A) 4s **(1)** from the 2nd and 3rd platoons of Company C and Company B, 776th Amphibious Tank Battalion, armed with 75mm howitzers **(2)**, fired on Japanese reverse slope positions around ridges that overlooked Highway 2 **(3)**. The LVTs were about 750 yards offshore from Balugo **(4)**.

After firing 2,500 high-explosive and smoke rounds against the Japanese, and combined with infantry pressure from the US 17th and 184th Infantry regiments, the stalemate was eventually broken. The LVTs would also fire on Balugo and turn north to bombard Tabgas. This action helped Krueger's forces in dispersing Japanese defenders and it allowed the Americans to move north and eventually link up with the 77th Infantry Division, which would land up the coast near Deposito on December 7. The success of this combined sea and land attack allowed the American units to push forward to the key objective of Ormoc.

Ridge was only the beginning; 7th Infantry Division units would have to eject their determined foe across similar terrain for days in the Battle of the Ridges.

To push ahead, Krueger employed a familiar tactic: an amphibious operation to bypass heavy enemy defenses. The 776th Amphibian Tank Battalion, with landing vehicle, tracked (LVT) A-4s, employing 75mm howitzers, smashed Japanese positions north of the 184th Infantry Regiment These craft deployed, about 1,000 yards (900m) offshore, west of Balugo on December 5. From there, they hit targets where the 26th Division concentrated. LVT A-4 crews fired against the enemy in their reverse slope positions where 7th Infantry Division's artillery failed to reach. The LVT A-4s could now identify and fire hundreds of high-explosive and white-phosphorous shells on enemy positions in Tabgas, a town north of the Palanas River. The 7th Infantry Division crossed the Palanas River and fanned out from Shoestring Ridge. Krueger used the LVTs to advance up the coast, with infantry support. These waterborne carriers achieved surprise and fired point-blank against Japanese coastal positions, allowing Krueger to reach Albuera by December 8.

Kenney's slow progress in developing airfields continued to delay MacArthur's Luzon invasion. Without airfields, the ability to support the next operation at Mindoro slipped from December 5 to 15. However, Tacloban Airfield was now fully operational. Army engineers estimated they could do the same for Bayug and Buri. Bayug became home for the 110th Reconnaissance Squadron's P-40s on November 3. Similarly, fighter pilots started to use Buri on November 5. However, Kenney had to contend with the 35 inches (90cm) of rain that fell in the following 40 days. Coupled with poor drainage, soil conditions, and roads, Kenney had to abandon the fields. American air and ground units also started to leave San Pablo Airfield. This left the Burauen area without a working fighter airfield, but Bayug and San Pablo did have L-4 liaison aircraft. The closet operational airfield was Dulag, from where fighters had begun to operate on November 19. Engineers would develop another airstrip at Tanauan a month later. Land-based air power for any operation out of Leyte was still limited.

SUZUKI'S LAST GAMBLE: BURAUEN

Yamashita and Suzuki still had one option left. If the Japanese wanted to keep Leyte, they needed to counterattack. The IJA was not totally defeated yet and they continued to receive reinforcements and supplies. Japanese officers centered their attention on Burauen. Yamashita's headquarters issued an order on November 23 to take the Burauen airfields. They speculated if they could knock out these airfields, then the Americans could be defeated when they lost their air power. An IJA offensive, the *Wa* operation, using the 16th and 26th divisions and Japanese airborne forces, would try to take the airdromes. However, if Suzuki lost the 16th and 26th divisions, there would be no holding back the Americans.

Just before Suzuki's divisions struck east out of the mountains, the IJA's 2nd Parachute Group (composed of the 3rd and 4th Parachute regiments) would land on the Buri, Bayug, and San Pablo airfields for the *Te* operation part of the mission. These airfields had some American personnel, but possessed no combat aircraft; Kenney had largely abandoned the airfields since the rains began. Airborne forces would also attack Dulag and Tacloban.

US and Japanese positions and movements, December 4–21, 1944.

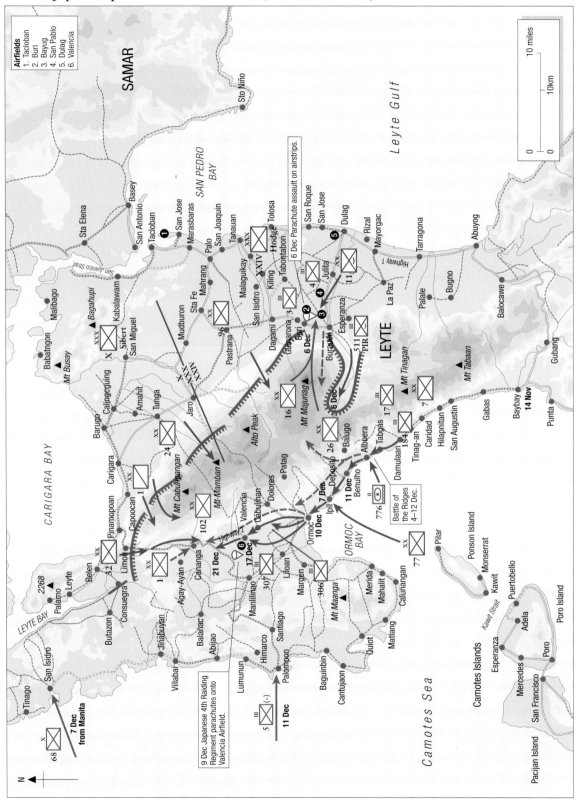

Preceding this attack were air strikes on the targeted airfields between December 1 and 3. Japanese officers planned for a diversionary IJNAF attack with ground operations in Limon that would keep the Americans busy from December 4 to 7. The exact date of the *Wa* operation or ground attack was uncertain, but staff officers estimated it would occur sometime between December 5 and 10. Yamashita also hoped to send his remaining air forces to control the skies the night before the ground attack.

Such Japanese airborne activities were not unique; early in the war, Japanese paratroopers had fought in Southeast Asia. In addition, Fourth Air Army officers had already attempted to knock out the Burauen airfields in late November in the *Gi* operation. Using 40 men from the Kaoru Raiding Detachment, four aircraft with ten men apiece were to land at the airfields to wreck planes and facilities with explosives. The planes left Manila early on November 27. Unfortunately for the Kaoru Raiding Detachment, some of the pilots dropped into the wrong locations. One pilot reached Buri, but the Americans shot the plane down. Others landed near Dulag and Abuyog airfields, but the *Gi* operation failed to meet its objectives.

Japanese ground forces faced challenges. The 16th Division originally numbered 10,625 effective personnel before A-Day. By December 2, Makino only commanded 500 men, who moved from the Dagami region to Buri. The 26th Division had landed at Ormoc, but had suffered losses in equipment and supplies from American attacks on the convoys carrying it to Leyte. The division still had to get into position for the attack. The 26th Division also had to wait until the 68th IMB relieved them to block the 7th Infantry Division from moving up the coast.

Yamashita determined X-Day, execution day, for December 5, but Suzuki reported his forces needed until December 7 to get into position. Yamashita agreed to the date and delayed the *Wa* operation a day with an attack on Buri set for 0630 on December 6. Despite the delay, the 26th Division was not in a position to fight. It dragged itself towards Burauen and later Bayug and San Pablo. Suzuki's operation soon started to unravel. Due to weather problems, the Japanese delayed the parachute attack by 24 hours, but the 16th Division did not receive the changed orders.

Makino's 16th Division finally reached Buri with about 300 men. The presence of Japanese soldiers awoke American aviation engineers, signal troops, and others at 0630 on December 6. The attackers routed the Americans, despite the lack of paratroopers. Paratroopers landed later that night and the Japanese took control of Buri the next day. However, out of 35 transports flying from Lipa, south of Manila, only 17 made drops on the evening of December 6. About 60 paratroopers arrived at Buri; the remainder dropped on San Pablo. Staff officers arranged for another wave of Japanese airborne forces to reach Leyte the next day, but weather forced its cancellation.

Relatively little has been written about the Japanese parachute arm, which first fought in combat on Sumatra in the Netherlands East Indies on February 14, 1942. The Japanese used IJA Raiding Regiments and IJN's 1st and 3rd Special Naval Landing Forces in the defence of Leyte. Yamashita deployed the IJA Raiding Regiments against Burauen and other locations that would eventually fall to the US advance. (US Army)

Although the Japanese attack caught the Americans by surprise, it failed to retain total control of Buri or San Pablo. The Americans at both airfields reorganized their forces and defended their positions. A mixture of engineers, artillery gunners, 11th Airborne Division glider infantry, 38th Infantry Division units, and a tank battalion pushed out the Japanese. MacArthur had released his reserve 38th Infantry Division to the area to counter any attack around Burauen. The Americans retook San Pablo on December 11. No Japanese paratroopers survived. At Buri, Japanese forces tried to push forward to Bayug, but there were no friendly forces on the airfield as planned. The 16th Division was a shell of itself and the 26th Division could not reach Burauen in strength. Japanese forces had run out of weapons and ammunition and relied on captured American munitions. Suzuki ordered a retreat. Without any additional forces, the Japanese departed and tried to combine with the 26th Division troops that had pushed west to Burauen. The combined *Wa* and *Te* operations had failed.

To make matters worse for the Japanese, the American 77th Infantry Division, which had been transferred from Nimitz's command to MacArthur's on November 15 and had arrived on Leyte on November 23, had conducted an amphibious landing south of Ormoc.

FROM DEPOSITO TO ORMOC

With the Mindoro invasion delayed, MacArthur could now conduct operations in the Ormoc area with naval forces. The air situation had improved over Leyte for MacArthur. Air units arrived for action, such as the five Marine Corps fighter squadrons that flew to Leyte on December 4.

The X Corps was still attempting to make headway around Mount Cabunganan. Despite the Japanese 1st and 102nd divisions' weakened condition, however, the American effort to forge across the area was labored. Enemy resistance was still strong and advancement slow. The 77th Infantry Division amphibious landing was intended to break this log-jam. MacArthur wanted greater Sixth Army progress and the capture of Ormoc could force Suzuki's units to collapse.

The Japanese hung on. Yamashita continued the *TA* operations. With the Americans moving north with the 7th Infantry Division, *TA-8*, with the 68th IMB, was supposed to land at Albuera, but Fifth Air Force P-47s' strafing and bombing of *TA-8* forced its withdrawal to San Isidro near Leyte's northwest tip, where it unloaded 4,000 men on December 7. The Japanese landed too far from current operations to support Suzuki immediately. Although the Fifth Air Force sank all of the transport ships, the Japanese still delivered troops and supplies.

With the continuing erosion of Japanese air and naval power in the Camotes Sea, the rise of American naval power, and the availability of amphibious capability, Krueger prepared the 77th Infantry Division for a landing on December 7 at Deposito, just south of Ormoc. Japanese observers had witnessed a large convoy of 80 ships off Baybay moving north at 0305 on December 7. The only immediate response was that Japanese aircraft managed to attack the invasion fleet, with the Fourth Air Army sending 50 aircraft from its 2nd Air Division and 12 bombers from the 5th Air Brigade, and the 4th Air Division sending 20 suicide aircraft. First Combined Base Air Force ordered 56 aircraft to sink the convoy. The Japanese air attacks only damaged two destroyers, which later sank, and a transport, at a cost of 36 planes. Japanese shore batteries also opened fire on the convoy at 0634, but Kinkaid's destroyers responded. The defenders failed to stop the invasion.

American forces streamed ashore almost unopposed at 0707 using six destroyers and Fifth Air Force aircraft for fire support. TG 78.3 carried two regiments, the 305th and 307th Infantry, which came ashore on two beach areas. Kinkaid conducted minesweeping and destroyer patrols before the landing to ensure a smooth invasion. Suzuki now faced a major threat. His forces had earlier recognized the need to establish defenses near Ormoc, but did not have time or the labor to do so. As the 77th Infantry Division consolidated its position, the threat to the Japanese at Burauen and units holding down the 7th Infantry Division increased since they could be cut off. Krueger's 11th Airborne Division could force out the 26th Division and the remaining 1st Division forces from Burauen. The paratroopers might cross the mountains and force Suzuki to withdraw from the Ormoc Valley.

Suzuki could assign the 68th IMB from San Isidro to reinforce the 1st Division, but its help was problematic. This action would allow the Thirty-Fifth Army to continue its defensive operations against the US X Corps and protect the Ormoc Valley. Further Japanese reinforcements only delayed the inevitable. Although IJA divisions throughout Leyte fought on, they were ready to collapse due to combat losses, lack of supplies, and fatigue. The 16th Division had fewer than 200 effective soldiers. IJN destroyers and escorts were only able to send one last *TA* convoy to Palompon, on Leyte's northwest coast, after Ormoc fell, arriving on December 11. The only reinforcements immediately available were the 4th Raiding Parachute Regiment, about 500 men, who could help defend Valencia, the remaining airfield in Japanese hands.

Once the 77th Infantry Division troops had come ashore, they moved north on Highway 2 to Ormoc. Suzuki called on the Matsui Shipping Unit service troops to defend Deposito. With almost all IJA ground combat units engaged against the Americans, the 77th Infantry Division advanced with little effort to Ipil. Still, the Americans encountered stiffened resistance near Camp Downes, about a mile (1.6km) south of the port city. Infantrymen encountered a deadly combination of pillboxes, dugouts, and obstacles manned by the Mitsui Shipping Unit, 77th Regiment soldiers, 30th Division elements, and others. Japanese troops stood ready with automatic weapons, antiaircraft guns, and field artillery supporting the infantry. The 26th Division's 12th Independent Infantry Regiment deployed to Ormoc, but its commander had to release a battalion to support the Camp Downes area defense and allow time to prepare against the Americans. Heavy fighting slowed the American advance. Still, Krueger broke through Camp Downes on December 9 and reached Ormoc the next day.

While the 77th Infantry Division snaked its way north, the 7th Infantry Division tried to take Deposito. Japanese officers in the 13th Independent Infantry Regiment realized two American divisions had trapped them. They retreated east through the mountains and met up with the 26th Division remnants. Suzuki's men tried to stem the enemy advance into Albuera. Unfortunately for Suzuki, the 7th Infantry Division largely quelled enemy opposition and there was little chance of stopping Krueger now, especially with the 77th Infantry Division in Deposito. Krueger could also pursue the Japanese through the mountains with the 7th Infantry Division and link up with the 11th Airborne Division.

JAPANESE PARATROOP RAID ON SAN PABLO AIRFIELD (PP. 80–81)

The Japanese command on Leyte believed that if American air power was grounded, and by capturing their airfields, then the IJA could retake the island. Lieutenant-General Suzuki Sosaku approved a combined ground and airborne assault on the airfields near Burauen. Ordering the 16th Division and paratroopers from the 3rd and 4th Raiding regiments to strike the airfields, the IJA soldiers attempted a night paratroop raid on San Pablo.

On December 6, around 1840, 250–300 paratroopers jumped from Mitsubishi Type 100 Ki-27s **(1)**, and despite antiaircraft fire managed to land on the airfield. Limited American forces from the

11th Airborne Division resisted, but units consisting of headquarters staff, engineers signal, and service troops could not hold out against the Japanese combat paratroopers. The IJA paratroopers **(2)** destroyed Piper L-4 Grasshopper observation aircraft **(3)**, a jeep **(4)**, and supplies **(5)**. Japanese mocked the American defenders of the airfield, yelling "Where are your machine guns?" **(6)** and other insults – a ruse to get the Americans to return fire. Eventually, the Americans recaptured the airfield with airborne infantry units. Following this defeat and one at nearby Buri Airfield, the Japanese retreated into the surrounding hills.

Suzuki had relatively few forces remaining to protect Ormoc. He could only muster about 1,700 soldiers, mostly service and support troops, against thousands of American infantrymen. The only combat forces came from the 12th Independent Infantry Regiment's Imahori Detachment, about 350 soldiers. These forces fought from entrenched positions. American soldiers had to clear individual pillboxes, which delayed progress in moving forward. Suzuki directed any 16th Division survivors to end the *Wa* operation and help Ormoc's defense. Although the Japanese defenders resisted, American forces secured one strongpoint at a time. Using tanks, flamethrowers, engineers, and rifle fire against pillboxes, the Americans slowly pushed out the Japanese. By the evening of December 10, the Japanese had abandoned Ormoc, their main supply base, and started to retreat north. Suzuki's only reasonable alternative was to regroup north of the city and join the rest of the Thirty-Fifth Army. Once the Japanese left Ormoc, the 16th and 26th divisions and the remaining units faced encirclement if the US X Corps managed to push south and rendezvous with the 77th Infantry Division.

Lieutenant-General John Hodge, XXIV Corps commander, received news of Ormoc's capture from the 77th Infantry Division's Major-General Andrew Bruce, who remarked: "Have rolled two sevens in Ormoc, come seven come eleven." These references to his division and the 7th Infantry Division and 11th Airborne divisions accurately represented the situation. Suzuki's force could only await the fall. The Fifth Air Force and PT boats mauled the last *TA* convoy sailing to Palompon on December 11 and 12. Yamashita planned to send the 10th Division's 39th Infantry Regiment, recently arrived on Luzon, to the Carigara Bay area on December 16–17, but he later cancelled the operation. With no means to put up an effective resistance, the 16th and 26th divisions started to collapse. There future orders were to "interrupt" any American activities.

Securing the Ormoc Valley

After fighting intensely against Suzuki's forces, the 7th and 77th Infantry divisions required resupply. Japanese air attacks had damaged several landing ship, medium (LSM) and LCI vessels in December, including two LSMs sunk near Baybay on December 4 and another during the Deposito landings. These vessels were essential for resupplying these units. Nimitz's Seventh Fleet staff recommended that supplies arrive overland by truck from the east coast to Baybay. LSMs and LCIs would then transport these to Ormoc. Krueger disagreed since this would delay getting ammunition and rations to his soldiers. Unfortunately, the number of LSMs and LCIs available was limited. This curtailment of the resupply effort severely restricted artillery and mortar ammunition fire. It also limited the ability to carry the 77th Infantry Division's Sherman medium tanks to the field.

With the deteriorating Japanese situation in the Ormoc Valley, the X Corps forces moved

Field Artillery battalions lent their weight against Japanese positions and forces on Leyte. This 155mm M1A1 Long Tom gun had a crew of 14 and could fire rounds up to 14 miles (22.5km) away. A typical M1A1 crew could prepare and fire 40 100-pound rounds an hour. Crews could load armor-piercing, high-explosive, white phosphorus, or chemical munitions. (US Army)

Japanese soldiers were adept at launching and conducting night attacks against American positions throughout the campaign. As a result, Krueger's units frequently required indirect fire support from artillery, as demonstrated here by this 155mm howitzer. Lack of sufficient air power also forced army ground units to rely on artillery for night and day operations. (National Archives)

south. Krueger assigned some of his forces against the 68th IMB at San Isidro. The 24th Infantry Division moved to the Calubian area, northeast of San Isidro. The 96th Infantry Division, with Filipino forces, climbed west across the mountains towards Valencia. Helping Krueger was the weakened condition of Japanese forces. Japanese soldiers positioned in the Limon began to run out of food and ammunition. The 32nd Infantry Division bypassed enemy positions instead of confronting them head on. By December 12, American units struck IJA artillery units south of Limon. The log-jam of enemy resistance started to break. The IJA's 1st and 102nd divisions slowly pulled back. The American 1st Cavalry Division and 32nd Infantry Division initiated the mop-up of enemy resistance in the rear areas, but they were clearly making progress south. American forces on Samar overcame most of the remaining Japanese opposition. Later, some mopping-up was necessary to ensure the Japanese would not oppose American shipping in the Visayans.

The leading American force, the 77th Infantry Division, made strides towards entering and taking Ormoc. They headed north on December 12 after being resupplied. Using their artillery fire support, bulldozers, flamethrowers, and tanks, and in intense house-to-house fighting, the Americans slowly cleared the city. Krueger's capture of the port city had sealed Suzuki's fate.

The last major holdout for Suzuki was Valencia. If the 77th Infantry Division could seize Valencia, then the Ormoc Valley would be in American hands. Instead of using frontal assaults, Bruce employed two regiments to flank the Japanese. They moved west initially. The 306th Infantry veered around the Japanese on Highway 2 and then towards Valencia. Meanwhile, the 307th pushed west and positioned itself near San Jose, south of Valencia's airfield. From those positions, Bruce could take the city and he could punch north to rendezvous with the X Corps heading south and corral the rest of the Thirty-Fifth Army.

Suzuki still hoped to recapture Ormoc, although it was an unrealistic proposition. With dwindling forces and supplies, the Thirty-Fifth Army planned to conduct operations with reinforcements landing at Palompon. The Fourth Army Air Force had dropped the 4th Raiding Regiment units into Valencia Airfield on December 9. These paratroopers reinforced the Imabori

The final moves, December 21–25, 1944

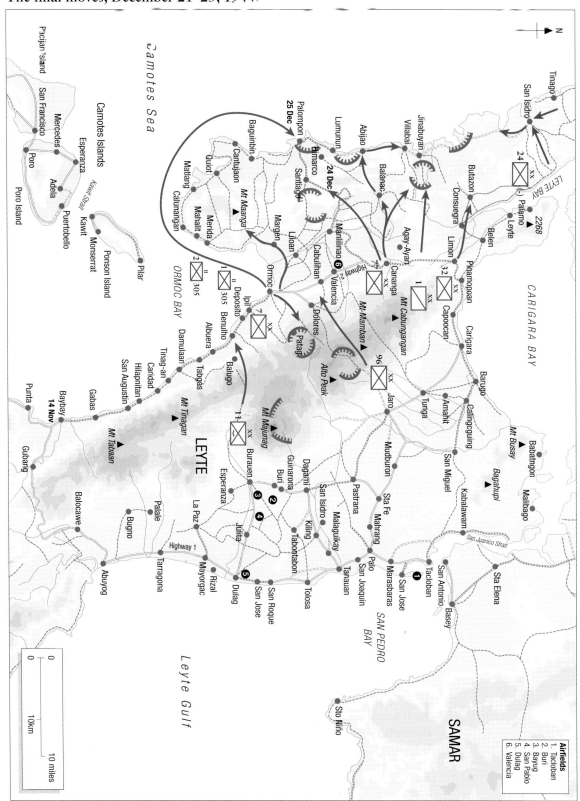

Detachment and could support this counterattack. Other forces were also available. Japanese units from the Imabori Detachment, 77th Infantry, and the recently arrived Ito Naval Landing Unit were to move south by December 15 and then contest the Americans north of Ormoc by December 17.

Coincidentally, the American 307th Infantry Regiment had moved just south of the Valencia airfield by December 17. The 306th had also advanced above Ormoc and could envelop Suzuki's forces. The Thirty-Fifth Army altered its plans again and avoided entrapment; they had to escape north. By the 18th, Krueger's men controlled Valencia and the airfield. Suzuki relocated his headquarters to Libongo, north of Valencia on Highway 2. The Americans successfully separated Japanese units along Highway 2. While the fighting continued on Leyte, units from the 24th and 77th Infantry divisions detached from their positions on Leyte and conducted an unopposed invasion of Mindoro on December 15. Yamashita realized that Leyte had become a lost cause with Americans south of Luzon.

Yamashita told Suzuki to change his strategy from a force fighting for the decisive battle of the Philippines to one of "strategic delay." Worse, Yamashita directed Suzuki to "promptly plan for self-sufficient, sustained resistance" – he could no longer rely on any reinforcements or supplies. Yamashita had received orders from Tokyo to withhold three divisions slated for Leyte to defend Luzon, now threatened by MacArthur's landing on Mindoro. Suzuki withdrew to his only viable defensive location, the remaining port of Palompon, on December 19.

Conditions had worsened for the IJA's 1st Division and remaining units. At a Highway 2 command post, about 500 soldiers tried to shield the rest of the Thirty-Fifth Army from Krueger's forces as it retreated to Palompon. As the Japanese soldiers moved west, they awaited defeat. One Japanese soldier's account reads:

> I am exhausted. We have no food. The enemy are now within 500 meters from us. Mother, my dear wife and son, I am writing this letter to you by dim candle light. Our end is near. What will be the future of Japan if this island should fall into enemy hands? Our air force has not arrived. General Yamashita has not arrived. Hundreds of pale soldiers of Japan are awaiting a glorious end and nothing else. This is a repetition of what occurred in the Solomons, New Georgia, and other islands. How well are the people of Japan prepared to fight the decisive battle with the will to win?

THE LAST STAND: PALOMPON

Suzuki's objective was to force Krueger's divisions to remain on Leyte as long as possible. This gave Yamashita a chance to improve Luzon's defense. Unfortunately for Suzuki's remaining soldiers, Yamashita's orders were to delay strategically MacArthur's men, not retreat, nor escape. Poised against the IJA were the 77th Infantry Division and the X Corps. On December 21, elements of the 77th Infantry Division and the 1st Cavalry Division met on Highway 2. Now, all of MacArthur's forces could combine and strike the remaining Thirty-Fifth Army units.

One battalion from the 77th Infantry Division's 305th Infantry Regiment would advance along a snaking road from Highway 2 to Palompon. Like other American moves, this advance went through steep cliffs, a narrow winding road, many bridges, and highly defensible terrain. Hodges wanted to move quickly and planned to ship two battalions 38 miles (61km) using LVTs from Ormoc to Palompon. They would arrive on Christmas Day. As the 305th Infantry Regiment moved down the road to the sea, Krueger caught the Japanese between his men. The 305th cleared the Palompon road on December 30.

Once the Americans took Palompon, MacArthur believed Leyte would fall. MacArthur announced that all apparent organized resistance on Leyte had ended on December 25. The next day, he ordered the Eighth Army to relieve Krueger's Sixth Army and mop up the remaining Japanese. The Sixth Army left Leyte to prepare for future operations, to include Luzon's invasion. With no replacements or supplies, Suzuki's soldiers faced a slow death. Despite Japanese orders to fight on throughout Leyte, some soldiers deserted to Cebu. Lieutenant-General Fukue Shimpei, 102nd Division commander, planned to evacuate without permission to Cebu, but Suzuki arrested him. Japanese units still operated in northwest Leyte and around the hills south of Palompon. The Eighth Army would "mop up" the remaining 5,000 (according to Sixth Army estimates) Japanese forces on Leyte and Samar – still a considerable operation. However, the Eighth Army staff estimates differed: they believed 25,000 Japanese soldiers remained on both islands.

Suzuki finally realized that his forces could still participate in the Philippines' defense. He ordered evacuations to start near Abijao, north of Palompon, on January 12, 1945. The lack of ships, plus American air, sea, and submarine activity, reduced Suzuki's ability to evacuate to other islands. The escape attempts stretched out for months. Approximately 740 men eventually escaped. Suzuki died near Negros Island on April 16 after American planes strafed his boat.

The Leyte campaign involved 257,766 US Army personnel. After months of combat, 3,504 had been killed and 11,991 wounded. Japanese sources indicate about 60,000 to 70,000 personnel fought on Leyte. Tomochika, Thirty-Fifth Army chief of staff, made claims of losing 59,400 from all services on Leyte. Sixth Army officers reported that they killed 56,263 Japanese with 389 captured by December 26. The Eighth Army staff reported they had additionally inflicted 24,294 Japanese killed from December 26, 1944 to May 8, 1945. The actual Japanese losses are unknown.

Fighting on Leyte challenged both American and Japanese soldiers. Tough weather, terrain, intense periods of combat, supply, and other common problems made fighting difficult for all. Several Japanese snipers were killed in a firefight when sheltering from American troops. Snipers were a constant threat to American forces during the campaign. (US Coast Guard)

AFTERMATH

Throughout World War II, the American military effort benefited greatly from the American economic engine that allowed soldiers to operate effectively in all theaters. American industry provided great support to the military. Here an American water supply point on a Leyte beach, on October 21, allowed soldiers clean water, a must during the hot, humid fighting on the island. (US Army)

MacArthur's return to the Philippines was a success. American forces on Leyte now held a foothold to take Luzon, Formosa, and other targets. Conversely, Tokyo lost its gamble for a decisive battle for the Pacific. Japanese forces suffered heavily with up to 70,000 casualties, irreplaceable IJN warship losses, and the sacrifice of hundreds of aircraft and crews. Japan's defeat on Leyte further deprived Yamashita of resources for Luzon's future defense. Conversely, American forces demonstrated innovation and the ability to adapt to fighting in difficult terrain and environmental conditions, as witnessed by the use of amphibious operations to bypass Japanese strongpoints, for example. However, although Leyte provided a great victory for MacArthur, it was not without problems.

One of the most critical issues facing Krueger was establishing working airfields to support Fifth Air Force operations. Unfortunately, adverse weather, logistical problems, limited engineering capability, poor soil conditions, and conflicting requirements bedeviled Krueger's engineers in their attempt to build the necessary air facilities. Without these bases, Kenney and Kinkaid had to contest the Japanese for air superiority early in the campaign. Failure to control the skies allowed Japanese aircraft to attack facilities, forces, and counter MacArthur's attempts to stem enemy reinforcements into Ormoc. Close air support and interdiction efforts early in the campaign stagnated until Kenney could attain air superiority. The lack of air power inhibited Krueger's soldiers from advancing quickly.

The American logistical effort was a significant contributor to its military success in World War II. Unfortunately, a large quantity of supplies does little if it is not in the hands of soldiers. GHQ SWPA had sufficient logistics, but Operation *King II* happened two months earlier than

planned. The shipping, loading, and stockpiling of supplies were hurried and haphazard. Supply distribution to dispersed units fighting in difficult terrain and monsoon season was tough. Filipino labor, the use of LVTs, and other exigencies did support combat units, but these efforts took time to do so.

Throughout the campaign, American ground forces tended to operate mostly on or near Leyte's highway and road system. Krueger's divisions seemed road bound, which limited their ability to maneuver. The nature of the terrain, weather conditions, and logistical challenges certainly contributed to this situation. Unfortunately, this also helped the Japanese to defend against the Americans and contest Krueger's operations.

One of Krueger's criticisms leveled against his officers with regard to the campaign was their relatively slow progress in taking Leyte. For Krueger's part, he believed officers did not take the initiative to drive out the Japanese quickly. His officers did use maneuver, but they also conducted many frontal assaults that slowed offensive actions to a crawl. Krueger thought his officers relied too much on direct and indirect fire support. Certainly, this process took time and put additional strain on the logistical system for munitions. If contested, American officers would dig in and rely on artillery support to counter the Japanese, which certainly reduced casualties. Another criticism was that his officers seemed to avoid battle unless overwhelming force was brought to bear against the Japanese.

Although Washington had access to a host of intelligence capabilities, notably ULTRA intercepts, there were still gaps in determining Japanese intentions, force capabilities, and strength. This led to the GHQ SWPA belief that the Leyte campaign would be short. Suzuki caught MacArthur by surprise with the ferocity and determination of his soldiers to fight. Japanese reinforcements, albeit limited, undermined Krueger's ability to defeat Suzuki quickly. Additionally, the American assumption that the IJN would not fight in Leyte almost cost Kinkaid his invasion fleet. If Kinkaid's CVEs had been lost, then Krueger's troops would have suffered through even less air power and MacArthur's forces may have been isolated. Still, ULTRA allowed the Americans to gain valuable information about Japanese intentions and revealed that Tokyo had believed the fantastic numbers of claims about American losses. American intelligence analysts, on the other hand, could identify Japanese intentions, a valuable insight for MacArthur.

Another issue for MacArthur was that there was no single unified commander for the Leyte operation. Although Nimitz

Torrential rain in the Leyte Valley created all types of problems for military leaders. For the Americans, road and airfield construction, movement, and combat operations slowed due to poor conditions caused by mud. Motor transportation of supplies, personnel, and weapons became stalled. Unfortunately for the Americans, the Leyte operation occurred during the rainy season. (US Army)

"chopped" forces to the GHQ SWPA, not all units fell entirely under MacArthur's control. Halsey was "dual-hatted" with Nimitz issuing him guidance to his Third Fleet to destroy the remaining Japanese carriers. MacArthur could direct Krueger, Kenney, and Kinkaid (whom he called "My Ku Klux Klan"), but Halsey broke contact with Kinkaid and pursued the IJN's Combined Fleet. This situation caused major concerns about the command and control of units when setting campaign priorities that could have resulted in a disaster at Leyte Gulf and ashore.

Fighting with forces under conflicting goals and objectives created issues for MacArthur. He had to rely initially on air power not under his direct control when operating on Leyte. MacArthur had to repeatedly request that Halsey's carriers not leave the area to avoid stripping him of air support – Halsey's forces had to depart Leyte Gulf due to supply issues. This limited Krueger's air support to the Sixth Army since he had to devote his small force to gaining air superiority. Unity of command and communications problems also surfaced early for the Americans and almost created a disaster, with IJN surface forces penetrating Leyte Gulf. MacArthur could not stop Halsey searching for the Combined Fleet. Fortunately, Kinkaid's CVEs were able to fend off the IJN and provided some air support while Fifth Air Force deployed.

If Washington had issues coordinating command and control over the Leyte operation, Tokyo's problems were worse. Japanese services frequently planned and executed operations without adequate coordination. Issuing the *Sho-Go* orders, the IJN directed their forces to activate the plan independent of the IJA. Fighting the United States was a daunting task, but combat without coordination and without concentrating Japan's limited fighting capability all but ensured a Japanese defeat on Leyte. There was no single commander in charge of IJA and IJN forces on the island. The Combined Fleet fought and lost the Battle of Leyte Gulf without much concern about the IJA. Even between the IJA's Southern Army and Fourteenth Area Army, there were disputes on strategy.

Yamashita could count on only a few maritime transports to send reinforcements from outside and within the Philippines. As the Allied noose tightened around the Philippines with its growing air, naval and ground control, transporting Japanese resources to protect the island got tougher. Defending Leyte became the only plausible action with little possibility of conducting a successful counterattack by Suzuki. The limited operations that Suzuki did manage to conduct were completed by understrength, weakened, and ill-equipped forces. Any counterattacks conducted were too late or done in a piecemeal fashion; Krueger had established a presence on the island and there was only a remote chance of Suzuki ejecting him. However, the Japanese attempt to take the Burauen airfields did succeed temporarily, but this "success" only hastened the 16th and 26th divisions' annihilation. Tokyo was able to delay but not defeat MacArthur.

The Japanese government also succumbed to faulty intelligence. They believed their pilots and naval officers' highly inflated claims of American naval losses in Formosa and the Leyte Gulf. These fantastic victory pronouncements altered the IGHQ and Southern Army campaign plans. With the alleged losses to the American Pacific Fleet, Tokyo had confidence that she would best the Americans. Suzuki could slowly and methodically defeat the Americans, but the large losses of Japanese aircraft and ships took its toll. The IGHQ could not dismiss the huge Japanese casualties in Formosa, the Ryukyu Islands, the Philippines, and around her shrinking empire. Despite the reported American casualties, the IGHQ should have questioned how the Allies continued to conduct wide-scale operations.

Japanese planning for the *Sho-Go* operation set the primary military focus on where the Americans attacked first. The *Sho-Go* plans appeared inflexible and did not allow for any adaptive planning. Against an enemy like the Americans, this was deadly. Fortunately for Washington, the IGHQ could not overcome flaws to their strategy. If MacArthur or Nimitz struck at any other location, the Japanese would designate that area as the site to concentrate their forces for large-scale operations. What if the Americans conducted a large diversionary operation? Or attacked in the Philippines, Formosa, or Central Pacific simultaneously on a broad front? The Japanese would have to gamble and commit early to a particular area to defend, which was wishful thinking at best. Yamashita's foresight about using too many forces to defend Leyte was correct. With a defeat on Leyte, Tokyo would face problems defending Luzon – as would be demonstrated in the weeks that followed.

Selecting Leyte as the main point of defense also raised questions. Luzon was undoubtedly the main strategic prize for MacArthur; Leyte was merely a stepping stone to this. Then why defend Leyte? If the Japanese needed to defend Luzon later or transfer forces to another Pacific base, then it would require all available forces and resources to fight the Americans. IJA and IJN forces attached to Leyte weakened this effort.

Air superiority was a key component in dominating the Leyte operations. For the Japanese, the IJNAF and IJAAF fought the Americans to a standstill early in the campaign. However, they could not parlay their initial advantage to a permanent one. The Japanese did not attack, in mass, the Americans during the initial beach operations on Leyte. If the IJNAF and IJAAF could launch large numbers of bombers and fighters against the two invasion sites, then it could have affected combat and support operations for a longer period. Japanese air attacks were sporadic. If the Japanese pilots had attacked in mass early, they could have disrupted American operations at the invasion sites or contested Kinkaid's forces in the critical Leyte Gulf battle.

Despite problems for MacArthur on Leyte, the Sixth Army prevailed and led to further operations in the Philippines. The Japanese, defeated and forced to retreat, could only await an inevitable American onslaught. With several IJA divisions spent on Leyte, loss of aircraft, and little remaining naval support, Luzon's fate was sealed.

Taking Leyte presented the Allies some options. MacArthur could direct an invasion on Luzon and complete the conquest of the Philippines. Conversely, Nimitz had a stepping stone to Formosa. Certainly, the operations in Leyte allowed the Americans to reduce Japanese air power around the region,

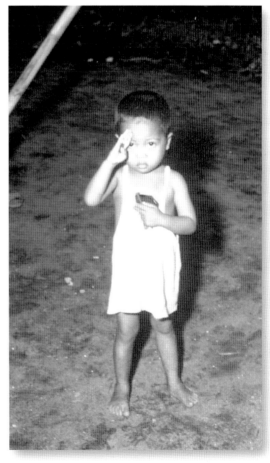

The American liberation of Leyte meant freedom for thousands of oppressed Filipinos throughout the island. Many Filipinos provided invaluable support to the Allied effort on Leyte from actively fighting the Japanese to distributing supplies to dispersed American units. A Coast Guardsman took this photograph of a boy on Leyte in 1945. (US Coast Guard)

especially on Luzon and Formosa. Fortunately for MacArthur, Nimitz would realize that a Formosa invasion seemed infeasible for a host of reasons: the lack of available shipping, port facilities, forces, loss of Chinese territory for B-29 bases, political impact, and progress in the Central Pacific all countered reasons to continue planning for Formosa. Instead, the JCS had directed MacArthur on October 3, 1944 to plan on a Luzon invasion. Although MacArthur justified the Leyte operation because it would provide air bases and logistics facilities for operations against Luzon, it was overstated. The long distances to Luzon and range of land-based fighters limited the worth of Leyte's airfields.

The American GI, throughout history, has always had a way to inject some humor into a situation. Here American soldiers try to put a bit of home on Leyte. This sign was probably erected somewhere near Tacloban Airfield on Cataisan Point. Fortunately for most GIs, they did not have to wait an additional 30 months to go home as the sign declares: the war would end in about 10 months. (US Coast Guard)

The Philippine islands conquest did not end the Pacific War immediately. However, the successful attack on the archipelago did tie down and destroy Japanese forces that Tokyo could have deployed elsewhere. More importantly, the Philippines' loss and its occupation allowed the Americans a major presence in a key area. The Allies could now cut Japanese access to vital raw materials that would severely disrupt the Japanese economy and seriously curtail Tokyo's military capabilities.

The Luzon operation would commence on January 9, 1945 with Krueger's landing of four army divisions in the Lingayen Gulf; it would become another tough struggle for MacArthur and Krueger and highlighted the savage nature of the fighting that would characterize the war's closing year. American forces retraced much of the route that the IJA took to eject MacArthur in 1942. MacArthur liberated Manila, the Bataan Peninsula, Corregidor, and other familiar Philippine locations. One of MacArthur's priorities was to free Allied prisoners of war and civilians throughout Luzon. In bitter fighting, the Americans had to advance through rubble in Manila, which resulted in substantial military and civilian casualties. Japanese forces punctuated the Manila fight with a number of atrocities. After Manila's fall, Yamashita could not retreat and so fought from the mountains in Luzon; he fought a tough, attritional campaign before eventually surrendering on September 3, 1945.

THE BATTLEFIELD TODAY

A visitor to Leyte can enter the island by car or bus from Samar through the San Juanico Bridge. Interestingly, one may travel north and south on Leyte via the Philippine–Japan Friendship Highway. Travel by ferry or ship to arrive at Ormoc city, still the island's main port, from Cebu city is another alternative. The fastest and most convenient method for reaching Leyte is by air. There are two major airports: Tacloban city is the primary destination of most commercial daily flights from Manila, while limited flights also arrive at Ormoc city.

Many of the island's cities have been developed or rebuilt since 1944–45. Still, one can drive on the Leyte road system that takes a visitor through the same routes as the American forces travelled throughout the campaign. Besides Tacloban and Ormoc, individuals can see the Leyte Landing Memorial on Red Beach near Palo. Here, one can view where General Douglas MacArthur and his staff landed on A-Day. The Philippine government has commemorated the start of the Philippines' liberation with statues of MacArthur and his staff wading ashore. There are also several local events celebrating the landings on Leyte throughout the month of October, especially near this memorial. In November 2013 Leyte was hit by a major typhoon that all but destroyed Tacloban city. Many of the buildings sustained damage, like the Price Mansion, now the College Assurance Plan building, where MacArthur established his forward headquarters. Other locations around Leyte's east coast were also damaged.

One can still observe many of the geographic features in the Leyte campaign. Visiting Palompon, Baybay, Damulaan, the ridges near Pinamopoan, landing sites near Palo and Dulag, and Leyte Gulf are possible. Unfortunately, urban and vegetation growth have obscured many battle sites and remaining Japanese entrenchments.

MacArthur ensured that he took the field on A-Day by visiting units on Leyte. While American troops tried to secure beachheads and move inland, MacArthur and his staff visited small units from the 24th Infantry Division on Red Beach. MacArthur was able to see firsthand the return to the Philippines. (US Army)

FURTHER READING

776th Amphibian Tank Battalion, *Operation Report Leyte Campaign, King II*, Secret (declassified), undated

Cannon, M. Hamlin, *Leyte: The Return to the Philippines*, Center of Military History, Washington DC, 1987

Chief of Naval Operations, *The Assault Landing on Leyte Island NAVAER 50-30T-6*, Department of the Navy, Confidential (declassified), Washington DC, December 1944

Drea, Edward J., *MacArthur's ULTRA: Codebreaking and the War against Japan: 1942–1945*, University Press of Kansas, Lawrence, KS, 1992

Eighth Army, *Report of the Commanding General Eighth U.S. Army on the Leyte-Samar Operation 26 December 1944-8 May 1945*, Secret (declassified), undated

General Headquarters Southwest Pacific Area, *Periodic Summary of Enemy Trends*, Secret (declassified), Military Intelligence Section, General Staff, various dates

Greenfield, Kent Robert (ed.), *Command Decisions*, Center of Military History, Washington DC, 2000

Hastings, Max, *Retribution: The Battle for Japan, 1944–1945*, Alfred Knopf, New York, 2008

Japanese Demobilization Bureau Records, *Reports of General MacArthur Japanese Operations in the Southwest Pacific*, Volume I, and Volume II parts I and II, Center of Military History, Washington DC, 1994

Kenney, George C., *General George Kenney Reports: A Personal History of the Pacific War*, Air Force History and Museums Program, Washington DC, 1997

Kreis, John, F. (ed.), *Piercing the Fog*, Air Force History and Museums Program, Washington DC, 1995

INDEX

Figures in **bold** refer to illustrations.

Abijao **49**, 60, 64, 76, 85, 87

Abuyog 11, 41, **46**, **47**, 49, 51, 56, 60, 64, 76, 77, 85

A-Day **26**, 33, 34, 35, 36, **37**, 39, 40, 41, 47, 51, 56, 77, 93
　A+1 39, 41; A+2 39; A+6 26; A+7 27; A+8 27; A+9 27; A+10 27; A+11 27; A+12 27

airfields:
　Bayug 42, **46**, 47, 49, 60, 64, **75**, 76, 77, 78, 85; Buri 11, 42, **46**, **47**, 49, 55, 60, 64, 75, 76, 77, 78, **82**, 85; San Pablo 11, 42, **46**, **47**, 49, 60, **64**, 75, 76, 77, 78, **82**, 85; Tacloban 26, 36, **37**, 39, 40, 41, 43, 49, 57, 58, 60, 64, 75, 76, 85, **92**; Valencia 11, 49, 60, 64, 76, 79, 84, 85, 86

Albuera 48, **49**, 51, 60, 61, 64, 68, 70, 75, 76, 78, 79, **85**

Allied forces, the 5, 6, 7, 9, 12, 16, 18, 21, 24, 25, 27, 28, 30, **37**, 91, 92
　Allied Air Forces 13, **14**, 19, 23; Allied Naval Forces 14, 23

artillery **6**, 17, **34**, 36, **37**, 39, 41, **42**, 45, 47, 48, 50, 54, 56, 58, 61, 62, 63, 65, 67, **68**, **69**, 71, **74**, 75, 78, 79, **83**, **84**, 89

Axis Powers, the 6, 25

Babatngon 45, **49**, 60, 64, 76, 85
battles:
　Battle off Biak **4**; Battle of Breakneck Ridge 60; Battle of Leyte Gulf 10, 23, 42, 43, 66, 90; Battle of Ormoc Bay 11, 63, **64**, 65; Battle of the Philippines 86; Battle of Philippine Sea **4**, 8; Battle of the Ridges 75, **76**; Battle of Shoestring Ridge **64**; Battle of Surigao Strait 43

Baybay 11, 26, 41, **49**, 51, 56, 60, 61, 62, **64**, 70, **76**, 78, 83, **85**, 93

Blue Beach 40, **46**, 47

bombers 6, 20, 22, **28**, 30, 31, 44, 58, **59**, 78, 91
　A-20 **20**, 51, 65, 67; B-25 **20**, 51, 56, 65, 66, 67; B-29 **5**, 6, 7, 20, 27, 31, 32, 92; dive **28**; heavy **8**, 20, 22, 31; light 22; medium 13, 20, 31, 56, 65; torpedo 43

Bong, Major Richard 57, 58

Breakneck Ridge 11, 60, 61, **62**, 63, 66, 67

Burauen 10, 11, **15**, 19, 26, 42, **46**, **47**, 48, 49, 51, 55, 60, 61, **64**, 67, 68, 70, 75, **76**, 77, 78, 79, **82**, 85, 90

Camotes Islands **49**, 60, 64, 76, 85

Camotes Sea 26, 51, 61, **64**, 65, 68, 70, 78

cannons 13
　20mm **57**; 75mm **20**, 56

Capoocan **49**, 50, 60, 61, 62, 63, **64**, 66, 76, 85

Caridad 49, 60, 64, 68, 69, 76, 85

Carigara 11, 26, **37**, **38**, 39, 44, 45, 48, **49**, 50, 51, 54, 60, 61, 62, **64**, 70, 76, 83, 85

Castilla **38**, 39

Cataisan Point **37**, 39, 43, **92**

Catmon Hill 11, 41, **42**, **46**, **47**, 51

Celebes **4**, 7, 22, 30, 66

China 5, 6, 7, 14, 15, 22, 31

communications **15**, 24, 36, 37, 50, 51, 55, 58, 90

Congressional Medal of Honor (CMH) 12, 57, 58

convoys 10, 11, 19, 26, 42, 48, **54**, 57, 58, **59**, 61, 65, 66, 70, 77, 78, 79, 83

counterattacks 7, **28**, 29, 30, 32, 35, **39**, 42, 48, 50, 61, 63, 66, 70, 71, 75, 86, 90

cruisers 14, 18, 32, 33, **34**, 36, **39**, **40**, 41, 42, 43, 44

Dagami 11, 42, **46**, **47**, **49**, 51, 55, 56, 60, 61, **64**, 76, 77, 85

Daguitan River **46**, **47**

Damulaan 11, **49**, 60, 64, 68, **69**, 70, 71, 76, 85, 93

Deposito 11, **49**, 60, **64**, **74**, 76, 78, 79, 83, 85

destroyers 14, 18, 32, 33, **34**, 36, **39**, 42, 43, 44, 59, 65, 66, 70, 79

Digahongan **46**, 47

Dulag 10, 18, 19, 20, 21, 26, **35**, 36, 40, 41, **46**, **47**, **49**, 51, 55, 56, 57, 60, 61, **64**, 70, 75, 76, 77, 85, 93

engineers 20, 25, 41, 57, 58, 65, **67**, 70, 75, 77, 78, **82**, 83, 88

entrenchment 39, 40, **42**, **47**, 48, 51, 54, 61, 63, 71, 83, 93

escort carriers (CVEs) 33, 36, **43**, 44, 57, 89, 90

fighters 20, 22, 23, 25, 32, 41, 43, 57, 58, 75, 78, 91, 92
　Grumman F6F Hellcat **58**; P-38 Lightning 57; P-47 **20**, 65, 78; P-61 **20**, 57

flamethrowers **6**, 56, 63, 67, 83, 84

flanking movements 50, 62, 63, 67

Formosa 5, 6, 7, 9, 10, 12, 16, 18, 20, 21, 22, 24, 25, 28, 30, 31, 32, 33, 35, 66, 88, 90, 91, 92

Guadalcanal **4**, 5, 14

Guam **4**, 27, 31

guerillas 17, 18, **22**, 25, 29, 50, 71

Guinarone **46**, 47

H-Hour 36, 39, 40

Halsey, Jr, Vice Admiral William F. **4**, 8, 9, 10, 14, 18, **19**, 22, 23, 25, 31, 32, 33, 35, **37**, 43, 44, 57, 58, 59, 65, 66, 90

Hawaii 9, 14, 18, **24**

Highway 1 **38**, **41**, **47**, 49, 56, 60, **64**, 76, 85

Highway 2 11, **37**, **38**, 39, 44, 45, 48, **49**, 50, 51, 60, 61, 62, 63, **64**, 67, **69**, **74**, 76, 79, 84, 85, 86

Hill 85 **38**, 39

Hill 120 **46**, 47

Hill 522 **37**, **38**, 39

Hill B **38**, 39

Hodge, Major-General John 16, 23, **46**, **47**, **49**, 60, **64**, 76, 83, 87

Hollandia **4**, 8, 10, 18, 30, 33

Honshu 5, 28

howitzers:
　8in. **45**; 75mm **19**, 56, **74**, 75; 105mm 50, 51, 71; 155mm 51, 71, **84**

Imperial Japanese Army (IJA) **5**, 6, 7, 8, 10, 11, **15**, 16, 17, 18, 21, 23, 24, 25, 26, 27, **28**, 29, 30, 34, **35**, 36, **37**, 41, 42, 44, 45, 48, 50, 51, 54, 56, 58, 59, 61, 62, **63**, 65, 66, 67, 70, 75, **77**, 79, **82**, 84, 86, 90, 91, 92
　Southern Army 14, 21, 23, **27**, 29, 34, 35, 66, 90; Fourteenth Area Army 10, 14, **15**, 21, 23, 29, 65, 70, 90; Thirty-Fifth Army **15**, 21, 23, 29, 35, 47, 48, 51, 61, 63, 70, 79, 83, 84, 86, 87; 1st Division 11, 48, 59, **60**, 61, 62, 63, 65, 66, 67, 70, 78, 79, 84, 86; 16th Division 7, 11, 21, 23, 25, 35, 40, **42**, **47**, 48, 51, 55, 56, 59, 61, 75, 77, 78, 79, **82**, 83, 90; 26th Division 23, 48, 61, 65, 68, 70, **74**, 75, 77, 78, 79, 83, 90; 30th Division 23, 35, 48, 61, 79; 41st Infantry Regiment 35, 48, 50, **54**; 102nd Division 23, 48, 50, 61, 67, 70, 78, 84, 87; 16th Division 7, 11, 21, 23, 25, 35,

40, **42**, **47**, 48, 51, 55, 56, 59, 61, 77, 78, 79, **82**, 83; 9th Infantry Regiment 23, 41, 45, **46**, **47**, 51, 55; 19th Infantry Regiment **37**, **38**, 39, 50, 63; 20th Infantry Regiment 23, 41, **46**, 55; 33rd Infantry Regiment 23, 37, **38**, 39, 41, 48; 49th Infantry Regiment 66, 67

Imperial General Headquarters (IGHQ) 9, 21, 27, 28, 32, 33, 34, 35, 59, 66, 90, 93

Imperial Japanese Army Air Forces (IJAAF) 16, 18, 21, 22, **28**, 29, 32, 34, 36, 44, 57, 65, 66, 91
　Fourth Air Army 21, 22, 23, 35, 77, 78; 2nd Air Division 21, 22, 23, 44, 78; 4th Air Division 23, 78

Imperial Japanese Navy (IJN) 5, 7, 10, 16, 18, **19**, 21, 23, 24, 25, 26, **28**, 29, 30, **32**, 33, 34, 41, 42, **43**, 44, 48, 59, 62, **65**, **66**, 70, 71, 79, 88, 89, 90, 91

Imperial Japanese Navy Air Forces (IJNAF) 16, 18, 21, 22, 23, 29, 32, 35, 36, 44, 57, 65, 66, 77, 91
　First Air Fleet **22**, 44; Second Air Fleet 22, 23, 44

independent mixed brigade (IMB) 21
　54th IMB 21, 23; 55th IMB 21, 23, **49**, 50; 57th IMB 48, **49**, 50; 68th IMB 21, 23, 48, 61, 77, 78, 79, 84

intelligence 21, 22, **25**, 26, 27, 45, 59, 65, 67, 89, 90

Japan 5, 6, 7, 9, 13, 17, 22, 24, 25, 27, 31, 34, 66, 86, 93

Jaro 11, 45, 48, **49**, 50, **54**, 60, 61, **64**, 67, 76, 85

Kenney, Lieutenant-General George C. 8, 10, 13, **14**, 16, 19, 20, 23, 25, 30, 40, 41, 44, 57, 58, 59, 61, 65, **67**, 75, 88, 90

Kiling **47**, **49**, 60, **64**, 76, 85

King, Admiral Ernest 6, 7, 9, 25

Kinkaid, Admiral Thomas **4**, 10, 14, 18, 19, 23, 25, 31, **33**, 35, 36, 39, 42, **43**, 44, 57, 58, 70, 79, 88, 89, 90, 91

Krueger, Lieutenant-General Walter **4**, 10, 11, **13**, 16, 17, 23, 25, 26, 36, **41**, 44, 45, 48, 50, 51, 54, 55, 57, 58, 59, 61, 62, 63, 66, 67, 70, 71, **74**, 75, 78, 79, 83, **84**, 86, 87, 88, 89, 90, 92

Kurita, Vice Admiral Takeo 42, 43, 44

Kyushu 5, 23, 28

Labiranan Head **42**, **46**, 47

Labiranan River **46**, 47

landing craft **24**, 33, **34**, 36, **39**, 40, 45, 65
　landing craft, infantry (LCI) **39**, 45, 83; landing ship, medium (LSM) 83; landing vehicle, tracked (LVT) **17**, **19**, **74**, 75, 87, 89; LVT A-4 **19**, 75

La Paz 45, **49**, 60, 64, 76, 85

Leyte Gulf 10, 14, **22**, 26, **28**, 33, 34, 35, 41, 42, 43, 44, 45, 50, 51, 57, 58, 66, 90, 91, 93

Limon 11, 44, **49**, 60, 61, 63, **64**, 66, 67, 76, 77, 84, 85

Luzon **4**, 5, 7, 10, 12, **13**, 14, **15**, 18, 20, 22, 23, 24, 25, 26, 28, 29, 30, 31, 32, 34, 35, 42, 44, 58, 59, 65, 66, 75, 83, 86, 87, 88, 91, 92

Macarthur, General Douglas **4**, 5, 6, 7, **8**, 9, 10, 11, **12**, **13**, **14**, 15, 16, 17, **18**, **19**, 20, 21, 22, 23, **24**, 25, **26**, 27, **28**, 29, 30, 31, 33, 34, 35, **37**, 39, 40, 41, 42, **43**, 44, 50, 55, **57**, 58, **59**, 61, 63, 65, 67, 70, **71**, 75, 78, 86, 87, 88, 89, 90, 91, 92, **93**, **94**

machine guns 13, **47**, 48, 50, **82**
　.50-caliber 56, 57

Makino, Lieutenant-General Shiro 21, 23, 55, 77

Managasnas 62, 66

maneuvers **17**, 26, 55, 62

Manila 10, 12, 13, 15, 21, **22**, 23, 35, 58, 59, 63, 65, 66, 77, 92, 93

Manus Island 10, **18**, **24**, 33

Marasbaras **39**, **49**, **60**, **64**, **76**, **85**

Mariana Islands **4**, 7, 21, 27, 28, 29, 30, 31

materiel 17, **29**, 34, **36**, **42**

Midway 5, 14

Mindanao **4**, 7, 8, 9, 15, 24, 25, 26, 28, 29, 30, 31, 35, 43, 58, 59

mines 26, 34, 35, 56
landmines 26; minefields 63; minesweeping 10, 18, 26, 33, 35, 79

Mitscher, Admiral Marc **4**, 31, 32

Morotai **4**, **8**, 9, 10, 13, 19, 25, 30, 31, 35, 41, 57, **59**

mortars 36, 37, **39**, **47**, 48, 55, 56, 61, 63, 67, **68**, 70, 71, 83

munitions **14**, 17, **19**, 20, 33, 43, **51**, 65, 78, **83**, 89

New Guinea **4**, 5, 6, 8, 13, 14, 17, 19, 21, 22, 24, 28, 29, 31, 33, **58**, **59**

Nimitz, Admiral Chester 6, 7, 8, 9, 14, 16, **18**, 20, 21, 22, 23, **24**, 25, 26, 30, **31**, 32, 78, 83, 89, 90, 91, 92

operations 6, 7, 8, 9, 10, 11, 13, 14, **15**, 16, **17**, **18**, **19**, 20, 22, **24**, 25, **26**, **29**, 30, **31**, **32**, 33, 35, **37**, 41, **43**, 45, 50, 51, 59, 61, 62, 66, 67, 70, **71**, 75, 77, 78, 79, 83, **84**, 87, 88, **89**, 90, 91, 92
Gi 77; Operations Instructions 70 10, 26; Operation *King II* 25, **37**, 88; *Sho-Go* 9, 14, 21, **22**, 27, 28, 90, 91; *Sho-Go 1* 10, 28, 34, 35, 42, 58; *TA* 10, 59, 78; *TA-2* 59; *TA-3* 11, 65; *TA-4* 11, 65, 66; *Te* 75, 78; *Wa* 11, 75, 77, 78, 83

Orange Beach 40, **46**, 47

Ormoc 11, 27, 44, 45, 48, **49**, 50, 51, 56, 57, 58, 59, **60**, 61, 62, **64**, 65, 66, 67, **68**, 70, 71, **74**, **76**, 77, 78, 79, 83, **84**, **85**, 86, 87, 88, 93
Bay 11, **49**, 59, **60**, 63, **64**, 65, 66, **76**, **85**; Valley 11, 27, **37**, 44, 50, 51, 61, 62, 67, 79, 83, 84

Osmeña, Sergio 37, **40**, 44, **94**

Ozawa, Vice Admiral Jisaburo **4**, 42, 43, 44

Pacific Ocean, the 5, 6, 7, 9, 12, 13, **17**, 18, **19**, **24**, 27, **28**, **37**, 42, 57, 58, 88, 91
Central Pacific 5, 6, 12, 24, **31**, 91, 92; Pacific Ocean Area (POA) 7, 16, 20, 26; Pacific War 5, 14, 92; South Pacific 14; Southwest Pacific 6, 7, 12, 24

Palanas River 11, **68**, 70, 71, 75

Palawan Island 4, 31, 43, 59

Palo 23, **37**, **38**, **39**, 41, 45, **48**, **49**, **60**, **64**, **76**, 85, 93
River 37, 39

Palompon **49**, **60**, **64**, **76**, 79, 83, 84, 85, 86, 87, 93

Panaon Strait 10, 26, 41, 56

Palau Islands **4**, 7, 8, 10, 14, 28, 30, **31**, 35

paratroopers 11, 67, 77, 78, 79, **82**, 84

Pearl Harbor 7, 9, 14

Peleliu 4, 31

Philippines 5, 6, 7, 8, **9**, **12**, 13, 14, **15**, 16, 17, 18, **19**, 21, 22, 24, 25, **26**, 27, 28, 29, 30, **31**, 32, 33, 34, 35, 37, **39**, 40, 43, 59, 65, 66, 86, 87, 88, 90, 91, 92, **93**
Islands **4**, 6, 7, 18, **39**, 66, 92

Pinamopoan **49**, **60**, 62, 63, **76**, 85, 93

pillboxes 27, 35, **39**, **47**, 50, 51, 54, 55, 56, 79, 83

PT boats 43, **59**, 65, 83

reconnaissance 18, 22, 25, 30, 34, 35, 43, 67

Red Beach 36, 37, **39**, **40**, 48, **93**, **94**

reinforcements 7, 10, 11, 20, 21, 22, 23, 25, 30, 31, 32, 35, 41, 44, 45, 48, **49**, 50, 55, 57, 58, 59, 61, 63, 65, 66, 75, 79, 84, 86, 88, 89, 90

resupply 18, 20, 23, 32, 41, 57, 83

Roosevelt, President Franklin 7, 9, 12

Ryukyu Islands 18, 21, 28, 30, 32, 91

Saipan 4, 9, 15, 27, 29, 31

Samar **4**, 23, 26, 27, 41, 43, 44, 45, **49**, **60**, **64**, 66, **76**, 84, 85, 87, 93

San Bernardino Strait 28, 43

San Isidro **49**, **60**, **64**, **76**, 78, 79, 84, 85

San Jose 18, 26, **36**, **37**, **39**, **40**, **46**, **47**, **49**, **60**, **64**, **76**, 84, 85

San Juanico Strait 10, 26, **39**, 41, 44, 45, 48, **49**, **60**, **64**, **76**, 85

San Pedro Bay **38**, **39**, **40**, **49**, **60**, **64**, **76**, 85

Shoestring Ridge 11, **64**, **68**, **69**, 70, 71, **74**, 75

Sibert, Major-General Franklin 16, 23, **38**, **49**, **60**, **64**, 76

Suluan Island 10, 26, 34

supply 10, 13, 17, **21**, 25, **29**, **32**, 37, 41, 51, 83, 87, 88, 89, 90

Surigao Strait 14, 43

Sutherland, Lieutenant-General Richard 8, 9, **94**

Suzuki, Lieutenant General Sosaku 7, 15, **17**, **21**, **22**, 23, **27**, 35, 37, 42, **47**, 48, 50, 58, 59, 61, 63, 65, 66, 67, 70, 71, 75, 77, 78, 79, **82**, 83, 84, 86, 87, 89, 90

Tabgas **49**, **60**, **64**, **68**, **74**, 75, **76**, 85

Tabontabon **46**, **47**, **49**, 51, **60**, **64**, **76**, 85

Tacloban 10, 19, 20, 21, 26, **37**, **38**, **39**, 41, 44, 45, **49**, 55, 57, 58, **60**, 61, **64**, 65, 75, **76**, 85, 93, 94
City 12, **39**, 93; Valley 36

Tanauan **38**, **47**, **49**, 51, 55, **60**, **64**, 75, **76**, 85

tanks **16**, 20, 26, 45, 51, 55, 56, 61, 63, 67, 71, 78, 83, 84
barriers 35; crews 26; M-4 Sherman 37

task group (TG) 18, 25
TG-38.2 57; TG-38.3 **19**; TG-77.1 Flagship Group 18; TG-77.2 Fire Support Group 18, **34**, **39**; TG-77.3 Close Covering Group 18, **39**; TG-77.4 Escort Carrier Group 18; TG-77.5 Minesweeping and Hydrographic Group 18; TG-77.6 Beach Demolition Group 18; TG-77.7 Service Group 18; TG-78.1 Palo Attack Group 23; TG-78.2 San Ricardo Attack Group 23; TG-78.3 Panoan Attack Group 23; 79; TG-78.4 Dingat Attack Group 23; TG-78.5 Harbor Entrance Control Group 23; TG-78.6 Reinforcement Group 1 23; TG-78.7 Reinforcement Group 2 23; TG-78.8 Reinforcement Group 3 23; TG-79.1 Attack Group A 23; TG-79.2 Attack Group B 23; TG-79.3 Transport Group A 23; TG-79.4 Transport Group B 23; TG-79.11 Screen 23

Terauchi, Field Marshal/General Count Hisaichi 10, 14, 21, 23, 34, 35, 58, 59, 66

Tinagan **49**, **60**, **64**, **68**, **69**, **76**, 85

Tinian 4, 31

Tojo, General Hideki 9, 15, 27, 31

Tokyo 5, 6, 7, 9, 13, 14, 15, 21, 22, 24, 25, 27, 28, 29, 31, 32, 33, 35, 59, 65, 66, 86, 88, 89, 90, 91, 92

Tomoyuki, General Yamashita 10, 14, **15**, 23

Toyoda, Admiral Soemu 10, 34, 42, 44

transportation 15, **21**, 30, 31, 51, **71**, 89

transports 11, **18**, 29, 32, **33**, 35, 42, 59, **65**, 77, 90

trenches **39**, 54, 55, 62

Ulithi **4**, 18, **19**, 30, 31, 58

ULTRA cryptographic intercepts 7, 21, 22, **25**, 58, 65, 89
MAGIC (codename) 21, 22, **25**

US Army 5, **12**, **13**, **17**, **19**, 23, 87
Southwest Pacific Area (SWPA) **4**, 7, 9, 10, **12**, **13**, **14**, 16, **18**, **19**, 20, 21, 23, 24, 25, 26, 30, **37**, 41, 44, 58, 88, 89, 90; Sixth Army 10, 11, **13**, 16, 17, 18, 19, 23, 33, **39**, **45**, 50, 51, 56, 61, 62, 65, 66, 67, 78, 87, 90, 91; X Corps 11, 16, 17, 23, **24**, 26, 33, 36, **38**, **39**, **40**, 45, 61, 67, 78, 79, 83, 84, 86; 1st Cavalry Division 16, **18**, 23, **26**, 33, 36, **37**, **38**, **39**, **40**, **41**, 44, 45, 48, 50, 61, 62, 67, 84, 86; 24th Infantry Division 11, 16, 18, 23, 26, 33, 36, **37**, **38**, **39**, **40**, **41**, 44, 45, 48, 50, 56, 61, 62, 66, 67, 84, **93**; 34th Infantry Regiment **38**, 48, 50, 54, 62, 63; XXIV Corps 10, 11, 16, **17**, 23, **24**, 26, 33, 40, **41**, **46**, **47**, 48, **51**, 61, **69**, 83; 7th Infantry Division **6**, 11, 16, 23, 35, 41, 42, **46**, **47**, 51, 55, 56, 61, 62, **69**, 70, 71, **74**, 75, 77, 78, 79, 83; 96th Infantry Division 11, 16, 17, 23, 26, 40, 41, 42, **46**, **47**, 51, 55, **56**, 61, 67, 84; 382nd Infantry Regiment **46**, **47**, 51; 383rd Infantry Regiment **46**, **47**, 51; Sixth Army Reserve 16, 23; 32nd Infantry Division 11, 23, 30, 66, 67, 84; 77th Infantry Division 11, 16, 23, 67, **74**, 78, 79, 83, 84, 86; 305th Infantry Regiment 79, 86, 87; 306th Infantry Regiment 84, 86; 307th Infantry Regiment 79, 84, 86; 381st Regimental Combat Team 23; Army Service Command 16, 23; 6th Ranger Battalion 10, 16, 23, 26, 33, 34, 35; Eighth Army 11, 23, 87; Task Force 38 (TF-38) 18, 25, 31, 32, 65; Task Force 77 (TF-77) 16, 18, 31, 33, 34; Northern Attack Force, Task Force 78 (TF-78) 18, 23, 25, 31, 32, **33**, **39**, 65; VII Amphibious Force 10, 23, **33**; Southern Attack Force, Task Force 79 (TF-79) 18, 23, **33**; III Amphibious Force 10, 23, 33

US Army Air Forces (USAAF) 5, 6, 67
Fifth Air Force 11, 13, 16, 19, 20, 23, 25, **26**, 51, 57, **58**, 61, 62, 65, 67, 78, 79, 83, 88, 90; 49th Fighter Group 20, 41, 57; 421st Night Fighter Squadron 20, 57; 475th Fighter Group 10, 20, 57; 22nd Bombardment Group 20; 43rd Bombardment Group 20; 348th Fighter Group 20; 3rd Bombardment Group 20; 312th Bombardment Group 20; 345th Bombardment Group 20; 417th Bombardment Group 20; 3rd Air Commando Group 20; Thirteenth Air Force 8, 20, 23; 11th Airborne Division 23, 67, 70, 78, 79, **82**, 83

US Navy (USN) 5, 8, 11, **12**, 25, **28**, **32**, **33**, **34**, **43**, 44, 58
Pacific Fleet 14, 22, 90

Violet Beach 40, 41, **46**, **47**

warships **32**, 33, 35, 43, 70, 88

Washington 5, 6, 7, **12**, 13, 21, 22, 24, **25**, 30, **31**, 89, 90, 91

White Beach 36, **37**, **39**, **40**, 41

World War I 12, 13, 14

World War II 13, 57, **58**, 88

Yamashita, General Tomoyuki 10, 14, **15**, 21, **22**, 23, 34, 35, 48, 58, 59, 66, 75, 77, 78, 83, 86, 88, 90, 91, 92

Yellow Beach 40, 41, **46**, **47**